The
Examen
Prayer

The
Examen
Prayer

Ignatian Wisdom for
Our Lives Today

TIMOTHY M. GALLAGHER, O.M.V.

With a Foreword by
George Aschenbrenner, S.J.

A Crossroad Book
The Crossroad Publishing Company
New York

This book is printed on 30% recycled paper.

The Crossroad Publishing Company
www.CrossroadPublishing.com

Printed in the United States of America
The text of this book is set in 11/15 Sabon.
The display faces are Tiepolo and Trade Gothic.

Library of Congress Cataloging-in-Publication Data
Gallagher, Timothy M.
    The examen prayer: Ignatian wisdom for our lives today / Timothy Gallagher.
        p.   cm.
    Includes bibliographical references.
    ISBN-13: 978-0-8245-2367-1 (alk. paper)
    ISBN-10: 0-8245-2367-9 (alk. paper)
    1. Spiritual life – Catholic Church. 2. Prayer – Catholic Church.
3. Ignatius, of Loyola, Saint, 1491-1556. I. Title.
BX2350.3.G35 2006
248.4′6 – dc22

                                                            2006013662

7   8   9   10   12   11   10   09

Contents

Part Three
CONDITIONS

Foreword

That the unexamined life is not worth living stirs a variety of responses. Some people outright deny the truth of the statement because they see it as the death knell for any spontaneous lifestyle. Others would salute the statement's truth in theory, but concrete practice of the examen as inscribing that theory in the details of daily living does not take effect. This book of Fr. Tim Gallagher, however, goes far beyond theory in a compelling use of personal practice and actual experience. His treatment bridges the frequent divide between the truth in theory and daily practice in a human life. His personal, experiential treatment of the examen resolves this frequent incongruity and introduces a more mature phase of renewed understanding of the traditional practice of examen.

The use of personal testimonies to exemplify various aspects of the examen adds a persuasive experiential tone. The quotations here are neither artificial nor contrived. This is especially true in the explication of the dynamic development and interrelationship of the five steps of the formal examen prayer. Even more convincing than an extra exhortation on the part of the author, these third-party reports have an influence all their own.

In 1972 my article on consciousness examen was the fruit of an insight that had connected for me: the heart of examen is daily practice of discernment of spirits. Lifting it out of an overly negative and moralistic misunderstanding, I described a practice that was meant to be much more positive and personal. Examen was, first, a review of God's sustaining and endearing love touching our hearts in the immediacy of every day. It was also a look into the unique and intimately personal flow of our consciousness — not exclusive of, but beyond a mere noticing of external behavior.

The integration of examen and discernment of spirits was central to Ignatius's understanding. For this reason, examen was the essential daily prayer for Ignatius, never excusable for any reason. Fr. Gallagher has recently published a book on Ignatian discernment.[1] That book serves as an important backdrop for his treatment of the examen. In this present book he singles out one special day of Ignatius's spiritual experience as recorded in his *Spiritual Diary*. March 12, 1544, was a key day, a rich, very lively day, in Ignatius's discernment about the type of poverty God was determining for the new Company of Jesus. Throughout this book Fr. Gallagher makes ingenious use of the account of this one day. It provides live, unrehearsed experience to exemplify various aspects of the examen and, for this reader, it endears again that Jesuit founder, that brother, in his reverential concern to treasure all of God's loving communications.

Entry into a practice of examen that is regular and perduring is not easy for many people. They start to practice it because it seems important, but it just does not last. Sometimes a particular experience ripens our heart and crystallizes a desire that has been growing almost without our noticing it. This grace of desire, a desire for God, a desire to love God more carefully, more thoroughly, paves an effective entry into the practice of the examen. In this way, through the flaring forth of the graced desire for a more personal loving relationship with God in Jesus, the examen "finds us." Only such "being found" can initiate and sustain the practice of examen.

Without enough genuine desire for a life of love with God, self-willed determination can never fit the examen to our lives. Only love and its burning desire, sheer grace from God, can evoke, direct, and develop our hard work of practice of examen into an effective lifestyle. For this reason, our contemporary postmodern culture poses a challenge for the examen. In a recent article on postmodern spirituality, Timothy Muldoon makes the following claim about many contemporary young people: "But what is so utterly foreign to many is the experience of falling in love with

God. Religion, for them, is an intellectual exercise rooted in the individual conscience, rather than a response to a God who holds out a hand to say, 'Let's have an adventure!' "[2] In such a situation the examen can become an intellectual, ethical practice aimed at a necessary reordering of a fractured world. But it does not pierce deeply enough into the subtleties and central loving commitment of our hearts.

The examen is about love, a love that all our hearts yearn for, a love beautifully manifested in many human examples but, finally, a love beyond anything we can fully experience before death. However, this ultimately satisfying love registers *now* in delicate, subtle movements of heart. To miss or to take for granted such loving touches is to lose a personal inner richness of life. To miss such inner intimacy also affects both our vision of the external world and the liveliness of motivation for our involvement with that world.

The examen is not an inner-hearted focus that blinds and distracts us from the external real-world context of our daily lives. Genuine love in the heart is always affected by and has its own impact on our society of organized international relationships. Within this mutuality of influence, the examen can cut to the heart of our future as a civilization. Our inability to control the fury of violent impulses is slowly shattering the trust needed for any responsible civilization. Daily our communications media tabulate the details of death inflicted around the world by the whiplash violence of terrorism, of disappointed love, and of frustrated hopes whether in schools, families, or many other interpersonal situations.

Violent impulses will always be part of the entanglements of the human heart in an interpersonal world. And learning to control appropriately the fury of these impulses to violence has become civilization's most needed lesson. The examen's regular decisive practice of discernment is precisely a matter of impulse control in faith. No, examen is not some unhealthy individualistic interiority. Its focus is no less than God's desire for a renewed and reconciled universe of interpersonal relationships, compellingly revealed in the Risen Jesus.

The examen invites its practitioner into the "sorrow place" of the heart. Not an easy fun place, it is like a haunted house in the neighborhood of all our hearts. Guilt, failure, shame, sorrow, and inadequacy bordering on helplessness inhabit this place and easily frighten us into avoidance tactics for detouring around this haunted, fearful section of our hearts. But precisely in the center of that apparently haunted house, and in that place alone, lies the precious transformative gift of peace, the peace that God's forgiving love in Jesus offers to us all.

To keep that sorrow place boarded up and scrupulously boycotted marks our hearts in a variety of ways. We experience an inner lack of integration, we pine for a peace we know we have not found, and we feel a distracting disconnection in a lot of our ministry. Most of us need a friend to accompany us into this scary place and to help calm some of our fears because of an experience of the zealous peace concealed there, and now personally discovered. No wonder Fr. Gallagher in chapter 1 speaks of shying away from the middle part of the examen and needing someone, often a spiritual director, to lead him to the full prayer of the examen.

Though at first this sorrow place in the human heart seems enervating and destructive of self-confidence, finally it is recognized as a birthplace: for profoundly humble self-confidence, for true spontaneity in the Holy Spirit, and for unquenchable zeal to serve in gratitude. Grateful awareness of God's personal goodness to us daily guides us confidently into the smelting furnace of sorrow where the deceptive allure and painful helplessness of sin reveal anew the startling gift of God's forgiveness in Jesus. And from that encounter, the energy of hope propels us in readiness for the future of tomorrow.

I mentioned at the beginning that some people reject the practice of examen as contrary to any spontaneous lifestyle. The real issue of spontaneity, however, cuts deeper in faith into our hearts.

A superficial quick spontaneity is easy, but often neither maturely human nor profoundly spiritual. The real issue of human life is to be transformed into the spontaneity of the Holy Spirit. None of us has this by nature. Something must die and be reoriented if this new profound spontaneity is to be born. A whole asceticism of careful discernment develops this true spontaneity of the Holy Spirit. The examen plays a central role in the development and personal assimilation of this new identity. The examen, far from sounding the death knell of any spontaneous lifestyle, celebrates the flowering of a genuine spontaneity that gives hope to us all. This spontaneity of the Holy Spirit in our hearts is always oriented to the continuing renewal of our universe, mirrored in the Risen Jesus, companion and pilgrim with us all every step of the way.

Fr. Gallagher's book propels the understanding of the examen a giant step forward. I congratulate him and his hard work, which will bless every serious reader.

GEORGE ASCHENBRENNER, S.J.

March 12, 2005, Anniversary of the
Canonization of Sts. Ignatius
and Francis Xavier

Acknowledgments

I am deeply grateful to the many people whose generous assistance has made the writing of this book possible. I thank Joseph Schner, S.J., and the Jesuit Community of Pedro Arrupe House, Toronto, for their warm hospitality during the months of writing. I am grateful to the academic community and the staff of Regis College, Toronto, for their welcome and for their constant willingness to assist in any theological or practical need during my stay. I am grateful in a special way to Gill Goulding, I.B.V.M., for her encouraging accompaniment at every stage of the writing of this book. My heartfelt thanks go also to George Aschenbrenner, S.J., for the gift of his foreword and for his encouraging response to this project.

I am grateful to all of the following for reading the text as I was writing, and for their observations regarding it that have so greatly contributed to this book: Daniel Barron, O.M.V., Susan Dumas, Rose Blake, Harvey Egan, S.J., James Gallagher, Elizabeth Koessler, Thomas Kleinschmitt, O.M.V., Catherine Macaulay, Gertrude Mahoney, S.N.D., Germana Santos, F.S.P., Ernest Sherstone, O.M.V., Mary Rose Sullivan, and Monty Williams, S.J.

In a particular way I thank Claire-Marie Hart for her generous and expert aid in editing the manuscript, Carol McGinness for her invaluable help with word processing and with permissions to quote copyrighted material, and Bernadette Reis, F.S.P., for assisting in these matters with her technical expertise. I am especially grateful to my provincial, William Brown, O.M.V., for encouraging the project of this book and for providing the opportunity to write.

Finally, I wish to thank the many people who shared their experience of praying the examen and who gave permission to quote their stories in this book. I am deeply grateful to them personally and for the richness their sharing adds to this book.

I thank the following for permission to quote from the printed sources listed here:

The Catholic Edition of the Revised Standard Version of the Bible, copyright 1965, 1966 by the Division of Christian Education of the National Council of the Churches of Christ in the United States of America. Used by permission. All rights reserved.

Excerpts from the New American Bible with Revised New Testament and Psalms. Copyright © 1991, 1986, 1970 Confraternity of Christian Doctrine, Inc., Washington, DC. Used with permission. All rights reserved. No portion of the New American Bible may be reprinted without permission in writing from the copyright holder.

Excerpts from *The Psalms: A New Translation,* copyright 1963 by Ladies of the Grail, administered by G.I.A. Publications, Inc. All rights reserved. Used with permission.

Excerpts from *Consciousness Examen Review for Religious* by Fr. Aschenbrenner. Jesuit Center for Spiritual Growth 1972. Used with permission of Fr. Aschenbrenner.

Excerpts from *A Commentary on Saint Ignatius' Rules for the Discernment of Spirits: A Guide to the Principles and Practice* by Jules Toner, S.J., 1982. Used with permission. © Institute of Jesuit Sources, St. Louis, MO. All rights reserved.

Excerpts from *The Discernment of Spirits: An Ignatian Guide for Everyday Living* by Rev. Timothy Gallagher, O.M.V., used with permission of the Crossroad Publishing Company.

Excerpts from *Here and Now: Living in the Spirit* by Henri Nouwen used with permission of the Crossroad Publishing Company.

Excerpt from *In Praise of Horizontal Prayer* by Frank Moan, S.J., in *America* 192, no. 4681 (February 21, 2005). Copyright 2005, all rights reserved, reprinted with permission of America Press.

Excerpts from the poem "Love" by George Herbert, in *The Norton Anthology of English Literature,* ed. M. H. Abrams, used with permission of W. W. Norton and Company, New York and London.

Excerpts from Tim Muldoon, "Postmodern Spirituality and the Ignatian Fundamentum," *The Way* 44, no. 1 (January 2005), British Jesuits Campion Hall, Oxford, UK. Used with permission.

Excerpt from *St. Thérèse of Lisieux: Her Last Conversations* translated by John Clarke, O.C.D. Copyright © 1977 Washington Province of Discalced Carmelites, ICS Publications, 2131 Lincoln Road, NE, Washington, DC 20002 U.S.A. *www.icspublications.org.*

Excerpt from *The Gift of Peace* by Joseph Cardinal Bernardin (Loyola Press, 1997). Reprinted with permission of Loyola Press. To order copies of this book, call 1-800-621-1008 or visit *www.loyolabooks.org.*

Excerpt from *On Giving the Spiritual Exercises: The Early Jesuit Manuscript Directories and Official Directory of 1599,* Martin Palmer, S.J., used with permission: © Institute of Jesuit Sources, St. Louis. All rights reserved.

Excerpts from *Selected Poems & Letters of Emily Dickinson,* ed. R. Linscott. Used with permission granted from the estate of Robert N. Linscott.

Excepts from *The Selected Poetry of Jessica Powers,* published by ICS Publications, Washington, DC. All copyrights, Carmelite Monastery, Pewaukee, WI. Used with permission.

Excerpts from "Finding God in a Busy Day" by Fr. David Townsend, S.J., in *Review for Religious* 50 (January–February 1991). St. Louis. Used with permission.

Introduction

Spiritual questions

It was a six-hour flight, and three hours remained before landing. I read steadily as time passed. Then I encountered this sentence: "Growth in relationship with God occurs through mutual self-revelation."[1] I immediately stopped reading. Without fully realizing why, I instinctively knew that in those nine words I had found something of great importance. I read no further and, for the remainder of the flight, I simply pondered those words.

The whole sentence was about *relationship*. I knew that if someone asked me, "What is the most important thing in your life?" I would answer, relationship with God and with other people (Mark 12:29–31). This was a sentence about "relationship *with God*," the most fundamental of relationships and the foundation of all other relationships.

These nine words promised to teach me about something I desired to learn: about growth in my relationship with God. They promised to tell me how such growth *occurs*. I knew then that these few words spoke of something fundamental in my life.

They told me that growth in relationship with God occurs "through mutual self-revelation." As the miles slipped away, I thought about that phrase. Self-revelation, it said, was the path to growth in relationship with God. And that self-revelation must be *mutual* if the relationship is to grow.

A flood of questions then arose within me:

- How does the self-revelation of a hidden God (Isa. 45:12) occur?

- Where can I look for that divine self-revelation?

- How will I know that I have found it?

- How will I know that I have understood it well?

To some degree I had answers for these questions. God's self-revelation is found in the pages of the Scriptures, in the Church, in the created world around me, through the people and events of my life, and in "a still small voice" (1 Kings 19:12) that speaks in my own heart.

But further questions remained. Yes, God reveals, but how attentive am I to that divine self-revelation? How often am I attentive to it? Could I, like the disciples on the road to Emmaus (Luke 24:13–35), be in the presence of the self-revealing God and not know it? Not realize what God was saying to me? How *open* were my eyes to grasp that presence and that self-revelation (Luke 24:31)?

The questions were equally challenging when I considered the other direction of this mutual self-revelation:

- How much of *myself* had I revealed to God?

- How willing was I to reveal myself openly and fully to God?

- Were there resistances within me to such self-revelation before God?

- If so, did I know what they were?

- Had I thought about *how* I was responding to God's self-revelation? About what made it easier for me to respond? About what might hinder my response?

I knew that these were key questions and that if I desired growth in relationship with God, I needed answers to them. I needed theologically sound answers, but something else as well. I needed a way of *recognizing* the answers to these questions in the concrete, daily experience that we call "the spiritual life."

This is a book about such questions. It is a book about how to find concrete answers to them. It is a book about a *way of praying* that opens our eyes to God's daily self-revelation and increasingly clarifies for us our own responses to it. As this spiritual clarity grows, we gain a correspondingly greater freedom to respond and so to progress in our relationship with God. We find a path toward what our hearts most deeply desire: a growing relationship in love with God (Ps. 63:1), and so with the People of God.

> What is the examen? How do I pray it?
> Will it be helpful for me?

In our spiritual tradition, this way of praying is called the *examen*. Although it did not begin with him and is not unique to him, the examen is associated in a particular way with Ignatius of Loyola (1491–1556), who so richly experienced it and so ably taught it to others. He will be our spiritual guide in this book.

A practical book

This is a book for those who do not yet know the prayer of the examen and wish to learn about it. It is also a book for those who do know of the examen and desire deeper understanding of it. It is a book both for those who wish to learn and for those who wish to teach others the prayer of the examen. This book is, even more, for those who wish to *pray* the examen: those who wish to begin to pray it and those who desire to grow in a practice already begun, perhaps years ago.

This is a *practical* book. It seeks to answer questions such as these: What is the examen? How do I pray it? Will it be helpful for me? Is it possible in a life as busy as mine? What will assist me to pray it? What obstacles might I encounter in the practice of the examen? Can I overcome such obstacles? If so, how? What spiritual fruit will I experience in praying the examen?

The book begins with that *desire* for loving and growing communion with God, which moves us to desire the prayer of the examen (part 1). Here I will share something of the personal journey that has led me to write this book. I will also review Ignatius's own experience of the examen as he describes it in his *Spiritual Diary*.

With this foundation in place, I will then discuss the *practice* of the examen: how we actually pray it in daily living (part 2). Here I will present each of its five steps individually and then together as a flexible whole.

Growth through the prayer of examen depends on more, however, than these five steps alone. Various additional spiritual means, wisely adapted to our personal situations, assist in sustaining a growing prayer of examen. In the next section of this book (part 3), I will outline the *conditions* that foster a fruitful prayer of examen.

Every authentic and enduring relationship of love necessitates, at times, the courage to love. The examen, as a profoundly relational prayer, may call for courage of this kind at various points. A consideration of when this may occur and of how God calls us to growth through such *courage* is a further key element in this book (part 4).

Blessed spiritual newness, growing daily communion with God, increased ability to serve, and many other gifts of grace flow from the daily prayer of examen. In the final part of this book, I will describe the spiritual *fruit* that God gives us through the prayer of the examen (part 5).

Experiencing the examen

In this reflection on the examen, I will focus in a special way on the *experience* of this prayer. The examen has solid roots in Scripture and in our spiritual tradition, and I will return to these foundations constantly throughout this book. With these established, I will illustrate the actual *practice* of the examen —

the focus of this book — through ample reference to concrete experiences of it. I have drawn these from a variety of sources.

Some I have taken from a selection of spiritual writers. Primary among these is, obviously, Ignatius himself as he describes his own experience in his *Spiritual Diary* and elsewhere. I will cite many others, past and more recent — including Bernard of Clairvaux, Thérèse of Lisieux, Julien Green, and Henri Nouwen.

Others are what I might call "reflected experiences." I have employed this genre of experiences in part 2 — on the practice of the examen — as a means of illustrating the precise nature of each of its five steps. By "reflected" I intend the following: I have given a name to each of the "persons" mentioned (for example, Jean and Tom in chapter 3). The experiences described do not refer to a particular person of that name but reflect rather the experiences of the many people I have encountered in twenty-five years of spiritual direction, retreat work, and spiritual formation more generally. These experiences are drawn from reality and reflect very real spiritual situations. Each experience focuses on the particular step of the examen under discussion and is intended primarily to illustrate that single step.

The majority of the experiences cited, however, derive from interviews with persons who were willing to share their experience of the examen and who gave permission to quote their experience in this book. I have cited each experience with the explicit permission of the individual involved and under condition of a confidentiality that I have carefully respected. I have therefore quoted these persons without using proper names; they are indicated only according to their calling: "a married woman," "a priest," "a woman religious," "a man," "a married couple," and similar titles. Their stories have greatly enriched this book, and I am deeply grateful to them.

The writing of this book has been a grace-filled experience of learning about the examen in ways that I could not have anticipated before undertaking the task. The labor of reflection, the discipline of writing, and, especially, the witness of so many dedicated people have all deepened my esteem and desire for this prayer. I am thankful to God for this gift. It is the gift that I hope to share with you in this book.

An Outline of the Examen

This outline is based on Ignatius's presentation of the examen in the *Spiritual Exercises* (no. 43). I place it here as an introduction to all that follows; it may also serve, once the content of this book has been assimilated, as a practical tool in praying the examen.

Transition: I become aware of the love with which God looks upon me as I begin this examen.

Step One: Gratitude. I note the gifts that God's love has given me this day, and I give thanks to God for them.

Step Two: Petition. I ask God for an insight and a strength that will make this examen a work of grace, fruitful beyond my human capacity alone.

Step Three: Review. With my God, I review the day. I look for the stirrings in my heart and the thoughts that God has given me this day. I look also for those that have not been of God. I review my choices in response to both, and throughout the day in general.

Step Four: Forgiveness. I ask for the healing touch of the forgiving God who, with love and respect for me, removes my heart's burdens.

Step Five: Renewal. I look to the following day and, with God, plan concretely how to live it in accord with God's loving desire for my life.

Transition: Aware of God's presence with me, I prayerfully conclude the examen.

PART ONE

DESIRE

Chapter One

Discovering the Examen

*So I saw him and sought him; and I had him
and wanted him. And it seems to me that this
is how it is and how it should be in this life.*
— Julian of Norwich

A journey of thirty years

I first learned of the examen thirty years ago, early in my seminary training. During the novitiate, a year dedicated to special
formation in the spiritual life, we studied our spiritual tradition
and the different ways of praying it offers us, such as meditation
on the Scriptures, liturgical prayer, and spiritual reading. Among
these forms of prayer was the examen.

We learned that there were five steps in the prayer of examen:
we would *thank* God for the blessings of the day just lived, *ask*
for the grace to see and overcome our failings, *review* the day to
see our spiritual experience throughout it, *seek God's forgiveness*
where necessary, and then *plan* spiritually for the coming day.
The five steps seemed well-ordered, and this prayer made sense
to me. I wanted to learn to pray. I wanted a faithful and growing
life of prayer. And so I was willing to pray the examen as part of
my life of prayer.

Still, as I look back, I do not recall that the examen made
any notable impression upon me at that time. While I accepted
it, other forms of prayer seemed clearly more central, especially prayer with Scripture and liturgical prayer: the Mass and
the Psalms of the Liturgy of the Hours. I accepted the examen

29

as a normal part of a faithful life of prayer. I found it neither particularly burdensome nor especially important in my
spiritual life.

During my years in the seminary, I read Fr. George Aschenbrenner's well-known article on the examen and, like so many
others, was impressed by it.[1] When I think back to that time, I recognize that I was not equipped then to understand fully what he
wrote. But I liked what I read. The article presented an attractive
vision of the examen as an aid toward finding God throughout the
day. The examen was, Fr. Aschenbrenner wrote, "a daily intensive exercise of discernment in a person's life."[2] In those years the
reality signified by "discernment" was largely beyond my training
and experience.

> I suddenly realized how useful and even
> vital the examen is in the spiritual life.

Four years later I made the Ignatian Spiritual Exercises. The retreat was a powerful experience. Those weeks of abundant prayer
under the guidance of a retreat director were a wonderful time
of further learning about the spiritual life. Again the examen was
presented to me. Again, for me, the experience was essentially the
same. The prayer of examen seemed spiritually reasonable. I was
willing to pray it and did try to pray it. The examen continued
to be a part — but still a marginal part — of my overall life of
prayer.

I finished my seminary years and began my active ministry. A
pattern developed in my practice of the examen that would recur
for many years. For some months I would pray the examen in
the evening, at least for a few minutes. Then, at some point and
for varying lengths of time, I would weaken in this practice. On
occasion I would raise the issue of the examen with my spiritual
director. In times of retreat I would generally renew my resolve to

pray it. I would begin again, and the pattern would repeat. While I could have wished for a more fruitful practice of the examen, life was busy and this was not a major concern.

When I made that first Ignatian retreat, I immediately loved the richness of the Spiritual Exercises. I began working during my studies and after to learn all that I could about them. Not much later I was asked to guide Ignatian retreats, and requests continued to come. Quickly I realized that I could not accept these commitments responsibly without learning much more about discernment than I then knew. I began to study Ignatian discernment seriously. After a time I began, somewhat hesitantly, to speak about discernment with retreatants.

The response impressed me. The retreatants seemed to find that Ignatius explained their own spiritual experiences and that his practical counsels were of immense value for spiritual growth. For the first time I realized the power in Ignatius's teaching on discernment: noticing, understanding, and responding to the different spiritual stirrings of our hearts in a way that leads solidly toward God in daily living. I watched these guidelines give new hope and new freedom to retreatants. Often I would meet former retreatants who would tell me of the continuing blessings and hope that they found in Ignatius's teaching on discernment.

This led to something unexpected for me regarding the examen. If the examen was indeed, as Fr. Aschenbrenner had written years earlier, "a daily intensive exercise of discernment in a person's life," I suddenly realized how useful and even vital the examen is in the spiritual life; it was the way of bringing into daily life the spiritual power of Ignatian discernment that I was witnessing in the lives of retreatants. For the first time, I became profoundly interested in the examen.

I began speaking in retreats about the examen as the way to live Ignatian discernment beyond the retreats, in daily life. Eventually these talks developed into workshops for groups outside the setting of retreats. But I was never entirely at ease with the

way things were developing. Though I was speaking with conviction and sincerity about the importance of the examen, I still
struggled in my personal practice of it.

I now truly desired to pray the examen and hoped for the fruits
it seemed to promise — growing daily awareness of and communion with God. And something really was changing. Generally I
would dedicate a few minutes, sometimes more, to the examen
at the end of the day. What had changed for me was the discovery of the examen's first step: looking for the Lord's gifts in the
day and then expressing gratitude for them. I found that I could
do this, and that it made a difference. Recognizing, at the end of
the day, God's gifts to me during that day would often gently lift
my heart.

Gradually I found that I could pray the fifth step as well, looking to the next day and planning with the Lord how I would live
it. I began to find this helpful, especially when I needed to give
structure to the following day. The fifth point gave me a clearer
sense of what the Lord seemed to want of me and how to arrange
my priorities and my time for the coming day to meet that desire. I regularly shied away, however, from the intervening three
points: asking for light and strength, reviewing the day, and seeking forgiveness. Something had grown, but something was still
missing in my practice of the examen.

Daily fidelity to the examen remained an effort, even as I en-
thusiastically taught others of its importance. At one point, after
reviewing this situation yet again in a retreat, I asked my spiritual
director if we could discuss the examen in each of our monthly
meetings. During that year and beyond, we did so. Slowly I was
learning something else about the examen, something I now believe to be key: that we need another or others to walk with us
spiritually in the prayer of the examen.

This had become my situation with respect to the examen:
deepened understanding of its spiritual richness, real desire for
it, some growth in praying it — but still many of the same old

struggles. I felt the distance between what I was saying to others and what I was actually experiencing.

In those years I met a man whom I knew to be praying the examen faithfully and with spiritual depth. He seemed close to God, and the authenticity of his life of service was beyond doubt. His witness remained with me and showed me that a fruitful practice of the examen was truly possible. Still, he seemed to me a rare exception to the more common struggles with the examen. For most of us, I thought, some growth in the examen was possible; however, his deep daily communion with God through the prayer of examen seemed beyond reach.

But something else would occasionally happen. At times, when I was not looking for it, the examen would, in a sense, "find me." These were simply gifts of God's grace. A woman religious who had ceased praying the examen writes: "The interesting thing is that a few years ago I began to realize that each evening I was making an informal review of the day, going over it with God. The examen found me! And this tells me that the examen is an integral part of growth in the spiritual life." She is right.

One evening I went to a service of song and prayer in a university chapel. Friends had insisted that I go, and I went, partly to please them and partly out of curiosity. This evening of prayer came at a particularly dark moment in my life. At the time, I held a position of responsibility, and my work was going well. But I was withering inside. The toll on my energies had been heavy, and I did not know how to overcome the exhaustion, depression, and spiritual desolation that I was feeling all too frequently. This physical and interior heaviness had been developing for several years and, more than I realized, I was on the verge of collapse. I knew, though, that I was in serious trouble. I had tried every means I knew to resolve the physical, emotional, and spiritual darkness — more faithful exercise, ongoing prayer, times of rest away from work — and I had failed to find a way.

We entered the chapel at the university. It was packed with six to seven hundred people, mostly students, seated, standing,

overflowing into every corner of the church and into its vestibule.
The service lasted two and a half hours. I was quickly humbled
as I witnessed the sincere and profound prayer of many in the
church. Their prayerfulness was contagious, and I could not help
but begin to pray as well.

Two and a half hours is a long time when, suddenly, you are not
involved in responding to an urgent problem, not working hard
on the task at hand, not answering a phone call, not typing at
the computer, not involved in a conversation or preparing under
pressure for the next commitment. For the first time in a long
time, I was simply brought to a stop. As those hours passed in
that crowded church, I had no choice but to surrender to the
prayer that surrounded me.

I was both closely bound to the others surrounding me and, at
the same time, deeply alone with the Lord. I begged the Lord for
help, for light to see, for strength to act. And during those hours
I did see, for the first time and with great clarity, the nature of my
situation. I had to face my own inability to resolve my struggle.
I also saw clearly the steps I needed to take to make a change.
Most basically, I needed to let myself be helped. I needed to share
openly with certain persons, people of competence and wisdom
who knew me and knew what I was experiencing, and to allow
myself to be led.

When I returned home I went to the chapel. I sat there, journal in hand, and wrote down what I had understood during the
service. The next day I began to put it into practice. That evening
of grace was a turning point for me in many ways, and my gratitude for it only grows as the years pass. I think now that that
gift of grace and all that has flowed from it touched the deepest
reason for my remaining resistance to the examen. I think that
the examen becomes most profoundly possible when I accept my
own helplessness and my need to be led by the Lord. Then I deeply
desire to see and to follow that leading every day; then I know
that I *need* a daily prayer of examen that will help me to see that
leading.

That evening was a time when the examen "found me." Those two and a half hours were a prayer of the examen. For the sake of what we will explore in the rest of this book, I will describe that evening in terms of the five steps of the Ignatian examen, those steps that I had learned so many years earlier without fully understanding their richness.

As I prayed in the university church, I begged the Lord for light and strength (step two). I reviewed in prayer my situation of the moment and the related stirrings in my heart (step three). I planned with the Lord the steps I needed to take the next day (step five). Gratitude (step one) was already present in the initial peace that came with clarity. That gratitude is increasingly present to me as I look back on that evening, now with the awareness of the many blessings that have flowed from it. The fourth step (forgiveness) was not in my mind and heart that evening. Perhaps it was still too soon. Probably, at least in part, I still struggled to accept God's loving forgiveness for the respect-filled and restoring embrace that it is, rather than the further immersion in failure that I could all too easily feel it to be.

Experiences such as this also teach me that the examen is God's gift, that it really is a work of *grace* and not merely the fruit of human effort. They teach me that the examen is truly *prayer,* something we ask God to do, and not human achievement.

As time goes by I see more and more clearly why Ignatius so warmly recommends daily examen. Examen is our way of being regularly available to God so that divine light and love can heal our darkness and point the way toward spiritual growth. So much can change when I am open *every day* to hearing God's voice in this way.

The deepest desire of the human heart

I realize too why this specific form of prayer matters so deeply. Certainly the examen cannot stand alone as a form of prayer.

Desire for the examen is born of a deeper desire. That more fundamental desire is expressed, for example, in the words of Julian of Norwich quoted at the beginning of this chapter, and it is repeated throughout the Scriptures:

> O God, you are my God,
> for you I *long;*
> for you my soul is *thirsting.*
> — Ps. 63:1[3]

Loving desire for communion of life with the God who loves us is the root desire. Prayer with Scripture, liturgical prayer, spiritual reading, and the other forms of prayer feed this desire. But the prayer of examen is the specific searching *every day* to find where God's love is *active* this day, where God's love is *leading* today, to discern what within me may be resisting that leading, and to discover the growth to which God is calling me tomorrow so that this deepest desire can be increasingly fulfilled. Nothing in the spiritual life can replace a prayer that seeks this awareness of God's daily leading in our lives.

A woman told me of a practice of prayer that she began when she was five years old. No one taught her to do this; she simply began it on her own. God and the love of God for her were very real. Every night before going to bed, she would kneel at the window of her room and pray an Our Father. Then she would choose a specific teaching, something that her mother had said during the day — for example, "Avoid talking badly of others." And she would ask God: "Did I do that today?" If she saw that she had not spoken badly of others that day, she would be glad. If she found that she had done so, she would be saddened and would ask God's forgiveness. Then she would end her day, her heart in close communion with the God whose love she knew so surely.

She recalls one day when she and her friends had been outdoors running together. One girl could not keep up, and they had left her behind. She had seen the sadness on this girl's face. She says:

"When I prayed at the window that night, God told me that we should never use our strength and our gifts to hurt others, but always to help them." She has never forgotten what God said to her that night. The memory of and the desire to live that word of God still move her to tears today as she speaks of this.

That nightly practice of prayer, she says, was natural, spontaneous, and unself-conscious. It was just talking with the Lord.

She prayed that way every evening of her life into her twenties. And when in her thirties she first learned of Ignatian spirituality and of the examen, she found herself saying: "Lord, this is a home-coming. I have been doing this all my life, since I was a child of five. The word 'examen' is just a label for something I have always done."

The examen had "found" this woman too.

I think that the examen finds us because whenever a heart cries out, "O God, you are my God, / for you I long; / for you my soul is thirsting," this deepest desire awakens another desire: the desire to *hear* God's voice *throughout the day* and to *respond* as fully as our strength, our souls, our minds, and our hearts are able (Mark 12:30). This kind of heart wants to "stay awake" (Matt. 25:13), wants always to be watchful and alert (Mark 13:33) to discern the coming of the Lord it loves. This kind of heart desires to encounter the God who is Emmanuel (Matt. 1:23), who is with us *always,* hour by hour, every day of our lives (Matt. 28:20). Such a heart desires the prayer that Ignatius, in our spiritual tradition, calls the examen.

Here, as so often, Ignatius is expressing and giving practical form to a desire already present in our hearts. Though at times the cry of this desire may be almost buried under the weight of busyness and burden, this desire is always alive deep within us. When it remains unfulfilled, our hearts know that something important is missing; they yearn for new depth and for closer communion in daily living. Ultimately, *every* human heart cries out: "For you I long; / for you my soul is thirsting." In outlining the prayer of the examen, Ignatius is simply articulating something our hearts desire, something which, perhaps in less conscious and less consistent ways, they already do: they seek, in the richness, the confusion, the joy, the anxiety, the hope, the pain, the fear, and the wonder of daily living, the God who alone can fully satisfy their human longing. The Ignatian examen is simply a means, a wonderfully effective instrument, toward fulfilling that desire every day.

Learning about the examen

In writing this book I met a number of people who described their personal experience of the examen. You will meet these people in the pages of this book. Among them are persons of all callings: laypeople, religious women, priests, and married couples. I am profoundly grateful to each one of them. They have taught me much about the examen.

From them I learned that I had been wrong in thinking few people really do pray the examen faithfully and fruitfully.

- One *married woman* told of praying the examen for fifty years.

- Another, *a mother of four children,* spoke of praying it regularly since first learning of it seventeen years earlier.

- A *doctor* related his efforts to pray the examen for the past twenty-three years.

- A *married couple* described their practice, from the day of their marriage, of praying the examen together every night.

- *Priests and religious* would refer very simply to their many years of faithfully praying the examen.

At times my questions about such fidelity would even evoke a certain surprise; this daily praying of the examen seemed, to these persons, simply a spiritual given in each day's prayer. They considered this normal and common practice, and they could hardly conceive of life without the daily examen.

From these faithful people I learned also that I was not alone in my own mixture of desire and struggle with the examen. Some labored to pray the examen at all. Others found the examen initially awkward and only later discovered their personal path with this prayer. For yet others the examen touched deep places of woundedness; only when healing began did their practice of the examen become more hope-filled and then grow. Some who had prayed the examen faithfully for years desired greater depth in praying it and were unsure of how to find it. In this book we will address such struggles: their causes, their meaning in God's loving providence for our lives, and the steps that help to resolve them.

I find that when I am faithful to this
practice, many blessings enter my life.

The examen is still not entirely easy for me. I have needed the stimulus of teaching the examen and even more of writing about it to urge me to "surrender" to it more fully. Often enough, as the moment for the examen arrives, it is still a wrench to set aside my activity and review the day with the Lord. Sometimes I wait too long, and tiredness makes the prayer difficult. Even more deeply, I still, too often, resist the call to surrender control in my life and to allow the Lord to lead me. Will these struggles continue? If the past is any predictor of the future, they probably will.

But something has changed. Through the grace of studying, teaching, and writing about the examen, and above all through the witness of others so faithfully dedicated to it, I now know, as I did not thirty years ago, that the examen is not marginal in the life of prayer. I now better understand why Ignatius himself prayed it so faithfully and why he considered it even *the* key "spiritual exercise." I know that Ignatius has much to teach me through his personal experience and his writing about the examen. I know that he can help me grow in this prayer of spiritual attentiveness, which, beneath all my surface resistances, I really do desire.

I find that when I am faithful to this practice, many blessings enter my life. The parallel that Ignatius draws between physical and spiritual exercises is real (*SpirEx,* 1).[4] When I am exercising regularly, I come to desire this physical exercise, and I feel its absence when I omit it. Something similar happens with the examen. The more faithfully I pray it, the more I desire it and the more I miss it when I am too "busy" or too "tired" to pray it.

When I pray the examen faithfully, the times of this prayer become moments of peace in a hectic day. They link with other times of prayer, and I find it easier, though I am so often distracted, to be with the Lord throughout the day.

Through praying the examen, I become more aware of God's continual giving in so many ways during the day. Slowly, the gifts begin to speak to me of a very real love behind the giving.

I begin to notice "small" things that make a difference. I notice, for example, that an effort to reach out to a particular person gave me an uplift of heart. As I remember and review that experience, I discover to my surprise that I now feel less interior resistance to that person than before. Having realized this, I can plan to do the same again with this person and with others, if the Lord will give me courage. Something new has come into my spiritual awareness through the prayer of the examen.

I notice more quickly when I am anxious or pressing too hard and, as I share this with the Lord in the examen, I ask for light and strength to grow. This growth is not always easy.... I also learn about my life of prayer in general, about habits that help me to pray and about others that do not. Then I can try to make spiritually healthy adjustments.

Finally, I know that the little I have learned about the examen is like the first small, hesitant step through a door that opens into an endlessly expanding field of spiritual beauty. I know that further steps into that beauty are possible if I will continue to allow the Lord to lead me.

I know that Ignatius has walked there. He has entered through the door of faithful, repeated, daily examen and penetrated far into that spiritual beauty, finding God *in all things*. And he, uniquely in our spiritual tradition, has described the path: the prayer of the examen.

In the pages of this book, we will walk there with Ignatius. We will listen as he shares his own experience and then his teaching regarding the prayer of the examen. That experience and that teaching can open this spiritual door for us as well. The God whom we seek and for whom our souls thirst calls us through that door and awaits us there with the gift of spiritual awareness and the embrace of divine love.

Chapter Two

A Day with Ignatius

Morning by morning he wakens —
wakens my ear
to listen as those who are taught.
— Isaiah 50:4

A gradual growth

We will begin our exploration of the examen by accompanying Ignatius in his own daily experience of this prayer. We will walk with him through the hours of a day as he describes it in his personal *Spiritual Diary*. The day we will review, March 12, 1544, shows us Ignatius at age fifty-three, having long been dedicated to faithful service of the God he loves. At this point in his life, God's grace and Ignatius's own grace-inspired efforts have developed in him a finely attuned sensitivity to God's workings in his heart. As we will see, he is keenly aware, hour by hour, of God's leading and of his response, constantly seeking to follow that leading with his whole heart and strength (Matt. 22:37).

But Ignatius did not begin this way. His profound sensitivity to God's promptings developed only with time. As his *Autobiography* reveals, though his heart was generously given to God after his conversion in Loyola, times of uncertainty and darkness still lay ahead. On one occasion in those early months, faced with a choice and "weary of examining what it would be good to do, and not finding anything certain on which to base his decision," Ignatius simply allowed the mule he was riding to choose his road, accepting his mount's choice as a sign of God's will.[1] This

42

is, obviously, very much an Ignatius with much yet to learn about discernment and the examen.

During the months in Manresa that followed, Ignatius made unwise choices regarding his spiritual practices; only with reflection and the help of others would he acquire spiritual balance.[2] This process of growth continued, and Ignatius's awareness of and capacity to respond to interior spiritual promptings developed until he reached the maturity of discernment manifest in his *Spiritual Diary* of 1544. As we will note, even in 1544 his struggles are not absent.

Growth in the prayer of the examen for Ignatius, as for us, occurs gradually over the years. For Ignatius, March 12, 1544, represents the fruit of years of faithful prayer and receptivity to grace. His experience on that day, as described in his *Spiritual Diary,* is a privileged window into the power that a faithfully practiced examen yields in spiritual growth.

The day begins

On Wednesday, March 12, 1544, Ignatius awoke and, as was his custom, dedicated the beginnings of his day to quiet prayer. He was living in Rome at the time together with his fellow companions of Jesus. Later that day he would describe his "customary" prayer as it unfolded that morning:

> In the customary prayer I felt much devotion, and from the midpoint on, there was much of it, clear, lucid, and, as it were, warm.[3]

Ignatius's spiritual day opens with prayer filled with a sense of God, which becomes, after the "midpoint," increasingly abundant and warm, accompanied by a sense of clarity and light. His day thus begins with a glad awareness of God in prayer.

Blessed by this prayer, Ignatius turns to the day's occupations. Witnesses affirm that these were days of intense and almost overwhelming activity for Ignatius. His fellow companion of Jesus

Jerónimo Domènech, serving in those days as Ignatius's secretary, wrote to the companions in Spain, describing the community's activities in those weeks.[4] For four months, Jerónimo tells them, Ignatius had been especially ill; in fact, if he (Domènech) is writing, it is because of his desire to relieve Ignatius of one more task in this time of "his continual illnesses" (285).

> Even in this time of deep desolation, Ignatius is keenly attentive to his interior experience.

Notwithstanding his weakened physical condition, Ignatius is handling multiple concerns within and beyond the community. He is working to ensure sacramental assistance for the dying in the city of Rome, and is further occupied with establishing a house in the city to receive women in difficulty. The companions, at the request of city authorities, have welcomed several men into their house to assist these men in entering the Church; one of the men has caused Ignatius some pain before undergoing, with Ignatius's aid, a profound change of heart. They have given the Spiritual Exercises to a number of persons. The Holy Father has ceded the Church of St. Andrew to the companions, and work is underway to render the attached house more suitable for use. And, writes Domènech:

> Ignatius, when free of his infirmity, has been extremely busy. His spiritual labors continue to increase, among them the hearing of confessions, since he is charged not only with the household of the Lady [Marguerite of Austria] but with the household of the wife of the ambassador of Spain as well, and this often requires his presence. He is also occupied with striving to reconcile divisions among various persons in matters of great importance,[5] and continues to work on the

Constitutions of the Company, and similar matters as well.
(289–90)

This manifold activity in the city, however, is only part of
Ignatius's daily occupations. As leader of the Company of Jesus,
he must simultaneously guide the companions' widely expanded
activity in Europe and beyond: Portugal, Spain, Germany, Italy,
and India.

Clearly, Ignatius's spiritual experience on this Wednesday,
March 12, will occur in the midst of a whirlwind of occupations and of continual calls for his attention and energy. This is
the kind of day that has begun with his "customary prayer," a
prayer filled on this morning with "much devotion."

The Mass

Ignatius now approaches the central moment of his day: the celebration of the Eucharist. He reaches the chapel of the community
where he will celebrate the Mass; there, according to his custom,
he prepares himself in prayer. A first sign of spiritual disturbance
now surfaces:

> Once in the chapel, since I saw some persons hurrying down
> the stairs, I did not feel prepared to say the Mass and so I
> returned to my room to prepare myself. This happened with
> tears, and I returned to the chapel. (380)

The external source of this disturbance appears to be the bus-
tle of others in close proximity to the chapel, which was in an
"extremely small and poor" house,[6] where sound carried easily.
A reading of Ignatius's *Spiritual Diary* reveals, however, that such
externally induced disturbances generally manifest an already
existing interior trouble; is such the case here? What follows suggests at least that possibility. Ignatius renews his preparation for
the Mass, now with a perceptible sense of God's closeness, even

to tears, and returns to the chapel. He then begins the celebration
of the Mass:

> During one part of the Mass I felt much devotion and at
> times movements toward tears. During the other I struggled
> repeatedly with what I should do about finishing, since I was
> not finding what I was seeking. (380)

For many days now, Ignatius has been celebrating Masses
and praying, seeking God's light concerning the kind of poverty he and his companions should adopt. In these days he has
seen clearly that God is calling them to a life of complete poverty and total trust in the Father's providence. Ignatius desires
to find confirmation of this choice on March 12, and so conclude his discernment. He had hoped to receive such confirmation
through a profound experience of spiritual consolation in his
Mass this day . . . and it has not occurred. Consequently his heart
now struggles, unsure of how to proceed. Should he continue the
process of discernment? Should he consider it already concluded?

A *time of spiritual desolation*

Ignatius writes:

> When the Mass was finished and I was in my room after-
> ward, I found myself utterly deserted and without any help,
> unable to feel the presence of my mediators[7] or of the Di-
> vine Persons, but feeling so remote and so separated from
> them as if I had never felt their presence and never would
> again; on the contrary, thoughts came to me at times against
> Jesus, at times against another Person, finding myself con-
> fused with various thoughts such as to leave the house and
> rent a room in order to get away from the noise, or to fast,
> or to begin the Masses all over again, or to move the altar
> to a higher floor in the house. I could find rest in nothing,

desiring to end in a time of consolation and with my heart totally satisfied. (380–81)

This is a remarkable text! Now the early morning prayer's devotion and warmth have utterly disappeared. The spiritual struggle already evident in the Mass has deepened, and Ignatius enters into total desolation; he feels completely separated from God as though he has never felt anything of God and never will again. This is the same Ignatius who earlier this day experienced "much devotion" in prayer and tears of consolation in preparing for the celebration of Mass....

Thoughts begin to bombard him against the Lord whom he loves and to whom he has given his life — confusing thoughts, one after the other, all accompanied by a turmoil of heart. Ignatius notices them, individuates them, and records them in his notebook. Should he leave the house in order to find the quiet he needs to hear the Lord? Should he undertake a fast to seek the grace of a solution to his present confusion? Should he — a striking suggestion regarding a discernment already clear in itself — disregard his decision to adopt total poverty and begin the entire process of discernment over again? Should he consider celebrating Mass on a higher floor, away from the noise that has occasioned his present interior trouble? Ignatius writes: "I could find rest in nothing...."

The problem . . .

Even in this time of deep desolation, however, Ignatius is keenly attentive to his interior experience and perceives that a desire of his own is a factor in the struggle he undergoes. He is aware that he wishes "to end in a time of consolation and with my heart totally satisfied." Having noticed this desire, Ignatius does not simply move forward in his exploration of his spiritual experience; rather he sets himself to reflect consciously on this desire, considering whether there may not be something suspect in it:

Finally I examined whether I should continue in the discernment. On the one hand, it seemed to me that I was seeking to look for too many signs and that I wanted them given within a period of time or in the celebration of Masses which would end according to my satisfaction; the decision itself [about poverty] was clear and it was not clarity about the decision that I was seeking but rather that the discernment should end in the way that I desired. On the other hand, it seemed to me that if I ended the discernment in such distress, afterward I would not be happy about it, etc. (381)

And he finds that there is indeed something suspect about it. Ignatius recognizes that the discernment itself concerning poverty is clear and that his present turmoil has nothing to do with a need for further clarity in that regard. The issue is rather that he had set his heart upon experiencing a specific kind of consolation in the Mass, which would confirm for him that the process of discernment was indeed concluded.[8] When God did not give this experience of confirmation "according to my satisfaction" and "in the way that I desired," his trouble then arose. Ignatius's examination of that desire has proven richly fruitful; he has discovered the key to his present turmoil and indecision, and the way toward a solution begins to open.

The answer . . .

With new insight Ignatius reconsiders his desire for confirmation "according to my satisfaction":

Finally I considered that since there was no difficulty with respect to the decision itself, it would be more pleasing to God our Lord to conclude the discernment without waiting for or seeking further proof, and without saying more Masses for this aim. So I placed the matter in an election[9] and felt that it would be more pleasing to God our Lord to conclude. (381–82)

Although Ignatius now sees with clarity that simply to end
the process of discernment would be more pleasing to God, his
heart — and not his alone! — struggles nonetheless to relinquish
what is "according to my satisfaction":

> At the same time, however, I felt the wish within myself that
> the Lord would consent to my desire, that is, that I might
> finish the process in a time of great consolation. Once I rec-
> ognized that I felt this inclination and that this was different
> from what God desired, I began to note this and to strive to
> move my heart toward what was pleasing to God. (382)

Ignatius's first step in finding his way out of darkness and doubt
was to examine his interior experience and to *notice* a desire stirring in his heart. The willingness to reflect on that desire and so to
come to *understand* it was his next step toward freedom. But clarity itself, indispensably valuable as it is, is not enough. Ignatius
now engages in an *active striving* to move his heart toward what
God desires. As he does so, the desolation lifts and consolation
returns. Ignatius writes:

> With this the darkness gradually began to lift and tears
> began to come. And, as the tears increased, I felt all desire
> to say more Masses for this purpose disappear. (382)

Assaults ... and a firm response

Ignatius has found clarity of mind. He has sought to conform
the desires of his heart to the desire of God's heart in accordance
with this clarity. Turmoil and doubt have passed, and his heart
once again feels close to God. In this renewed closeness, Ignatius
is ready to conclude the process of discernment and to move forward in God's service. However, the spiritual vicissitudes of this
day are not yet concluded. Ignatius will note in himself three further assaults on this clarity as the day unfolds. He will reject each
of them quickly and firmly; in so doing his decision will become

increasingly rooted and his consolation will grow. These attacks, once resisted, are transformed into catalysts for growth in light and strength.

A first thought comes to Ignatius "to celebrate three Masses of the Holy Trinity as a thanksgiving" for the clarity and peace he has found (382). He recognizes in this apparently devout thought, however, a subtle temptation to continue with the Masses (and so with the discernment) rather than simply end according to the clarity he has received. Ignatius rejects this suggestion and writes that in so doing "I grew much in divine love with many tears" (382). A deep consolation fills his heart and remains with him for about an hour "with great interior satisfaction" (382).

Ignatius's spiritual struggles have borne great fruit.

A question subsequently arises in his mind as to whether he should conclude the process that evening or immediately. As Ignatius considers this, he notes that his tears of consolation cease. He understands that this question is not of God, and he resolves to end the process at that very moment. With great decision he writes simply: "Finished" (383), and the days of his discernment regarding poverty are concluded.

A morning of struggle and grace has passed — all of this in a morning! — and Ignatius now goes to his midday meal. This meal is the time of the final effort to undermine his discernment, and it leads to a moment of great spiritual insight. While he is at table, Ignatius senses the first slight beginnings of an attempt to raise doubts once more, rejects these immediately, and finds that "with this, all that I had decided was confirmed with tears of consolation and with all surety" (383). Soon after, "a quarter of an hour later" (383), Ignatius's eyes are opened to the whole pattern of the enemy's efforts in these days to remove his peace and undo his decision, and of the consolations that God has given to confirm him in his decision. His *Spiritual Diary* for March 12 ends in light, firmness of decision, and a warm sense of God's loving closeness. Ignatius's spiritual struggles of this day, his close attention to them, the insight to which this attentiveness has led, and his consequent striving to conform his heart to God's desire have borne great fruit. He is ready in a new way to love and serve the Lord.

"Is it really possible to live this way?"

What now of us? Is God's love any less active in the hours of our days? Is it any less crucial for us, than it was for Ignatius, to note God's stirrings in our hearts as each day begins, while we are at prayer, in the midst of pressing occupations, during a meal, and throughout the day in general? To perceive, like Ignatius, whether the desires we experience each day conform to God's desires for us?

Is it any less important for each of us to be *aware* of those movements in our hearts? To *understand* clearly how to respond to them? To strive like Ignatius to *act* according to the stirrings that are of God?[10] To notice and resist the stirrings that would turn us aside from God's purpose in our day? What will happen in our spiritual lives if we do live with such spiritual awareness, understanding, and action? What will happen if we do not?

If we were to write a spiritual journal for today or for the preceding days, what would we write? How much of our interior spiritual experience have we noticed? How much have we understood? How have we responded to it?

Our exploration of even a single half-day in Ignatius's spiritual experience manifests plainly why he considered prayerful attention to interior spiritual experience and the effort to respond wisely to it to be *the* key element of the spiritual life, the one "spiritual exercise" that must always be present in a day that seeks to be a lived "yes" to God's will. Such ongoing prayerful attention to our spiritual experience and to our response to it is the practice of the Ignatian examen, the subject of this book.

The practice of examen begins when the foundational desire of our hearts is to "seek and find the divine will in the disposition of our lives" (*SpirEx,* 1) and when we long for a means to embrace this will in the concrete circumstances of our everyday living. This practice begins when we perceive that our hearts are an arena where many different movements stir (*SpirEx,* 32), movements that we must prayerfully sift if we would follow those that lead to God and resist those that do not. This practice begins when, like Ignatius, we grasp the unique role that a faithfully made examen can play toward fulfilling this desire. More is involved in the practice of examen than desire alone, and this book will explore these further issues. But the root of the practice of examen will always be *desire:* a desire that is an awareness of the immense love of the God who is ever close to us, a desire enkindled within us when we wish to respond daily, moment by moment, to God's love, and a desire that is, finally, a gift to be sought in humble and trusting prayer to the God who promises that searching hearts will find their desire (Luke 11:9).

One day when I had concluded a seminar on Ignatius and the examen, a participant approached and asked: "Is it really possible to live this way?" It was the right question. It was the question of someone who understood the daily effort Ignatius had made to notice and respond to God's action in his life, someone who had seen the spiritual fruits this daily effort brought into Ignatius's life. How shall we answer that question? Is it really possible to live this way?

Ignatius himself lived this way, practicing the examen, and through his Spiritual Exercises he taught others to live this way. His example, like that of other figures of holiness, reveals to us that the power of grace can work great things in the human person, greater than we might have dared to hope. Can you and I live this way? Or, more precisely, is it possible for us to take further steps along the same journey that led Ignatius to such profound awareness of the spiritual stirrings in his heart? Can Ignatius's teaching on the examen, the spiritual exercise that fosters such awareness, assist us in taking such steps? Ignatius is convinced that it can. Many before us have found that such growth is indeed possible. Is there a way then to undertake fruitfully the practice of examen, wholly dependent on God's freely given grace and, at the same time, generously willing to employ our human energies for the task?

In his *Spiritual Exercises*, Ignatius describes the prayer of daily examen according to five successive steps: gratitude, petition, review, forgiveness, and renewal. In the second part of this book, we will explore each of these steps and see how they may be exercised flexibly toward this goal of growing spiritual awareness and response.

PART TWO

PRACTICE

Chapter Three

First Step: Gratitude

How He must love to be told that He is loved!
And the more we tell Him so, the more He loves us.
— Julien Green

"The highest grace and everlasting love of Christ our Lord"

The first step in the prayer of examen is, Ignatius writes, "to give thanks to God our Lord for the benefits received" (*SpirEx*, 43). Why does Ignatius choose *gratitude* as the first step of this spiritual exercise? Why the choice of this out of the many possible ways of beginning the examen?

This first step, a review of God's gifts during the day with the gratitude that arises from them, is born directly of Ignatius's own experience of God. Until the age of thirty, Ignatius gave little serious heed to spiritual things, and his life was far from model. At that point he was wounded in battle and, during his convalescence in Loyola, gave his heart to Christ. Already during that convalescence, Ignatius began to experience the outpouring of God's grace.[1] When he arrived in Manresa ten months later, this outpouring increased beyond all measure. God treated him, he says, "in the same way a schoolteacher treats a child, teaching him,"[2] one profound grace following upon another.

From the very start of his turning toward God, Ignatius experiences God as *giving:* giving immediately, the moment our hearts say "yes" to God's desire for relationship with us, giving abundantly, endlessly pouring out in gifts a love greater than our hearts can fathom. A phrase in a letter to a laywoman captures his image of the God he has encountered: "We will much sooner tire of receiving his gifts than he of giving them."[3] These are striking words — and a striking image of a God whose desire to give is so great that it exceeds our human capacity to receive. To his fellow companions in the Society of Jesus he writes: "I have no doubts regarding that highest Goodness who is so eager to share his gifts, or of that everlasting love which makes him more eager to give us our perfection than we to receive it."[4] Repeatedly, as a spontaneous expression of the sense of God that fills his heart, Ignatius begins his letters with the desire that "the highest grace and everlasting love of Christ our Lord" ever accompany and bless us. Ignatius's image of God as ceaselessly imparting gifts of love to us is classically expressed in his Contemplation for Attaining Love (*SpirEx,* 230–37). In this prayer we do nothing other than contemplate, from one perspective after another, the gifts of the God who "desires to give himself to me as much as he can" (*SpirEx,* 234). Is there any happier or surer way to grow in love than simply to consider the gifts — and the giving of self through these gifts — of one who loves us? We can readily understand why Ignatius affirms that such consideration unleashes within us a power of grace to love and serve the Lord "in all things" (*SpirEx,* 233) — in every aspect of our lives. What can we not undertake when we know that *we are loved,* loved concretely, loved by *this* person, loved in each of the hours of this day?[5]

For Ignatius then, the consciously chosen remembrance of God's gifts is not just a moment in a spiritual day or simply a devout practice considered generally advisable and helpful. It is the *heart itself* of the way he understands God and relates to God. The *only* God he ever knew from the first moment of his conversion was this God who constantly bestows gifts of grace upon us, revealing through these gifts the infinite love with which we are loved. When Ignatius tells us that the examen begins with gratitude for God's concrete gifts during the day, he is opening a

window into the deepest reality of our spiritual lives: God's un-
bounded love for us and desire for our response, in love, to the
love revealed in this giving.

In one of his letters Ignatius explains more at length his thought
regarding gratitude.[6] In speaking of what is for him the almost
unendurable thought of ingratitude, Ignatius energetically describes — both by negation and by affirmation — the unique
power of gratitude in our relationship with God and with each
other. He writes:

> May the highest grace and the everlasting love of Christ our
> Lord be our never-failing protection and help.
>
> It seems to me, in the light of the divine Goodness, though
> others may think differently, that ingratitude is one of the
> things most worthy of detestation before our Creator and
> Lord, and before all creatures capable of his divine and
> everlasting glory, out of all the evils and sins which can be
> imagined. For it is a failure to recognize[7] the good things,
> the graces, and the gifts received. As such, it is the cause,
> beginning, and origin of all evils and sins. On the contrary,
> recognition[8] and gratitude for the good things and gifts re-
> ceived is greatly loved and esteemed both in heaven and on
> earth.[9]

It would be difficult to express more strongly a sense of the
incomparable value of gratitude. If you and I were asked to name
the most unbearable of all evils and sins in this world, what might
we choose? If you and I were asked to identify "the cause, beginning, and origin of all evils and sins" in our world, how might
we reply? For Ignatius, who has become so conscious of God as
constantly pouring out gifts of love upon our world and upon
each one of us, the answer to both questions is utterly clear: it
is the simple *failure to recognize (des-conocimiento)* "the good
things, the graces, and the gifts received" from God, simply not
to know that there is a God who loves us and who is unceasingly,
even this very day, bestowing gifts of love upon us.

What will happen in our lives and in our world when the recognition (*conocimiento*) of these gifts begins to grow within us? When day after day we consciously choose to recognize these gifts and the Giver's love for us that is revealed through them? Then, Ignatius says, something "greatly loved and esteemed both in heaven and on earth" will come into our hearts, bringing great blessings into our lives. The first step in the practice of Ignatian examen is exactly this: "to give thanks to God our Lord for the benefits received" (*SpirEx,* 43) in the course of the hours we are reviewing — to *recognize* these gifts and, through them, God's personal love for us.

In its first step, then, the examen begins with what is most fundamental in our spiritual lives. When the Scriptures record the history of God's saving work in the world, the primary reality is always what *God does*. The people's response is vital to their relationship with God as salvation history unfolds, but it is never the first reality; that is always the work of God, who takes the initiative in leading the people toward salvation. And what God continually does, Ignatius says, is to pour out gifts upon this people, past and present. The first step in the examen consists of recognizing the *primary reality* that shapes our daily lives. Some examples will concretize what this might mean in practice.

An experience of gratitude: A day with Jean

Jean is a woman of faith, a married woman with children in college. Prayer has long been an important part of her life, and over the years her relationship with God has deepened. As time passed Jean found that she wanted communion with God not only in times of prayer but also during the active hours of her day with her family and at work. She spoke about her desire with a woman religious whom she knew, and the other woman suggested that Jean undertake the practice of daily examen. For several years now Jean has been making the examen daily and meeting regularly with the woman religious to discuss her experience of the examen. Jean finds that although the examen at times requires effort, it really is helping her to "find God in all things"[10] in the course of her day; thus her days at work and at home are increasingly spent in conscious relationship with the Lord as her heart has long desired.

JEAN IS GENERALLY most able to review her day prayerfully in the evening, and, when evening comes this day, she begins her examen. She lifts her heart to the Lord, and with the Lord she thinks back to the way her day began. Jean remembers how a remark her husband made at breakfast revealed to her that he was more worried than she had realized about a problem he would face at work this day. She quickly sensed that he needed her to listen as he put his concern into words, thinking the matter through and working toward his solution as he spoke. She knew that he rose from their breakfast gratefully, with a clearer mind, more ready to go to work. Now she thanks the Lord for the gift of that insight into her husband's need that morning. She thanks the Lord for the gift of the greater clarity given to her husband through her listening, for the gift of her husband's gratitude, and for the communication between them that blessed the day as it began.

On her way to work Jean stopped at the parish for Mass. During the Mass she presented her concerns to the Lord: her husband's worries about his problem at work, relational tensions in her own workplace as well, and her daughter's struggles with classes in college. The Gospel reading was the feeding of the five thousand (Matt. 14:13–21), and this Word of God spoke to her heart. She saw there a Jesus for whom the needs of the crowd mattered deeply and who walked among them as healer: a Jesus who would not allow the people to depart hungry and in need. Her heart lifted in strengthened hope that her needs also mattered to God and that God would not leave her and her family without help. She left the church with new energy for the day. Now she remembers that moment of grace and in gratitude gives thanks to the Lord for nourishing her spiritually as the workday was about to begin.

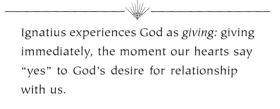

Ignatius experiences God as *giving:* giving immediately, the moment our hearts say "yes" to God's desire for relationship with us.

There were tensions in the office that morning, but Jean sensed that her relationship with one of the women was improving. Jean tried to reach out to the woman, and a brief conversation in mid-morning showed her that the other woman was aware of, appreciated, and was beginning to respond to her efforts. Jean now thanks the Lord for the gift of the improvement in this relationship and the hope it gives her of further improvement to come.

In the afternoon Jean completed a task that she had been working on for the past three days. She did it well and finished slightly ahead of schedule. This evening, as she remembers, she gives thanks to the Lord for the gift of a project successfully accomplished.

When she arrived home from work, her daughter called from college. There was tension in their conversation, and her daughter ended the call abruptly. The conversation left Jean with a heavy heart, unsure of how to relate to her daughter in her struggles with discouragement in college. Jean realized that she needed to talk about this and decided to discuss it with her husband and with a friend, also a mother, who had experienced similar difficulties with one of her college-age children. She thanks God for opening her eyes to the need to work toward newness in her relationship with her daughter.

At supper Jean and her husband shared the experiences of their day. As she remembers that sharing, she thanks God for the gift of the mutual support that both find in each other.

As Jean completes her contemplation of God's gifts to her throughout this past day, she finds that peace grows within her. With a quiet uplifting of her heart, she senses afresh how faithfully she is loved by the Lord in every facet of her life and sees clearly that the Lord has been close to her throughout the day; her desire to live consciously and continually in that relationship of love is deepened. Jean has experienced the blessing of the first step in the prayer of examen.

Confirmed in God's love: A day with Tom

Tom has been pastor of a parish for several years. Desiring to grow in his relationship with the Lord, he made an Ignatian retreat three years ago. Tom found that those days of prayer with Scripture did indeed bring him closer to God and desired that this relational newness would continue to grow. Tom shared his desire with the retreat director, and they discussed how he might integrate scriptural prayer into his daily life in the parish. The director also explained the practice of daily examen and suggested that Tom would find this prayer helpful in continuing his growth in relationship with God, according to his heart's desire. Tom decided to begin the practice of examen and has striven to pray it daily during the past three years. He has been pleased to experience how daily prayer with Scripture and ongoing examen have indeed fostered his relationship with God in a new way. The examen is helping him to sense God's loving presence and action not only in the Scriptures but also in the midst of a busy parish day.

Upon arising this day, Tom planned to make the examen after lunch, when he knew he would have a few quiet minutes before his first afternoon commitment. His lunch over, Tom now opens himself to the Lord's presence and, with the Lord, looks back over his morning.

Tom habitually begins his day with quiet time in prayer. In the preceding days prayer had been difficult, but this morning the Scriptures came alive and spoke to his heart; he felt the Lord's closeness as he prayed. Tom thanks God for the spiritual strengthening he experienced in that time of prayer. As he reflects he also recognizes that his prayer helped him respond to his parishioners this morning with genuine warmth. Again Tom expresses his gratitude to God.

After the morning Mass a parishioner approached Tom and thanked him for his homily. She told Tom that his brief explanation of the Gospel text was just what she needed to hear this day. Tom now thanks the Lord for the gift of that homily and how it helped this woman. He remembers that after she spoke with him and as he walked back to the rectory, he felt a sense of the goodness of his calling. For this too he offers thanks to the Lord.

Tom found himself able to listen and
respond well to the parishioner's need.
For this too he gives thanks to the Lord.

In mid-morning he was called to the hospital to assist a man seriously injured in an accident. When he arrived he found the man's entire family distraught and in pain. He listened to those who wished to speak with him, prayed with the family, stayed with them for the time they needed, and then left, promising to return later. He knew as he returned to the parish that his presence had helped them. Now he thanks the Lord for assisting him to serve these people compassionately in their suffering.

Driving back to the rectory still thinking of the pain these people were feeling, Tom suddenly realized how the coming Sunday's Gospel text could be applied to such trials in life. He now knows what the basic message of his Sunday homily will be and knows that it will help his parishioners. Tom expresses his gratitude to the Lord for this insight.

When Tom returned to his office he found on his desk a letter from a parishioner expressing angry disagreement with the way Tom is planning to organize the catechism program for this year. Tom's first response upon reading the letter was to become angry himself. When he was calm, Tom recalled that others also had expressed misgivings about the advisability of the proposed plan and recognized that he and the director of religious education needed to discuss these criticisms. He knows that the discussion will be helpful to them both and that whatever the final decision may be, this discussion will assist him in responding more wisely to those who disagree. He now thanks God for the gift of this initially upsetting letter.

Upon returning Tom also found a phone message on his desk. A speaker whom he had invited to give a talk in the parish had called to accept the request. Tom now thanks the Lord for this response and for the good this talk will accomplish in the parish.

Tom's final appointment that morning was with a parishioner who had asked to speak about a personal problem. Tom found himself able to listen and respond well to the parishioner's need. For this too he gives thanks to the Lord.

Tom concludes his review of God's gifts with a clear sense of how God has accompanied him in his priestly ministry that morning. Confirmed in his awareness of the Lord's love, he is strengthened in his readiness to serve the parish this afternoon. He will approach his pastoral commitments in the next hours with a deepened sense of the Lord's leading in the midst of his activity. Like Jean, Tom also has experienced the grace of the first step of the examen.

The practice of step one: Gratitude

In these examples, Jean and Tom chose to review God's gifts in chronological order from the start of the day until the time of the examen itself. Some people will find it helpful to practice step one of the examen this way.

There are other possibilities as well. On another day, as they make the examen Jean and Tom may find their hearts sponta-neously drawn to thank God above all for a specific gift that they have experienced as particularly significant that day: Jean's daughter, having done well in her semester finals, for example, calls to share her joy with her mother, or the evening with the speaker in Tom's parish is fruitful beyond his expectations and opens the way to further initiatives that will bless the parish. Jean and Tom may find that in step one of the examen, their hearts cen-ter spontaneously on these special gifts and they are less inclined to follow their customary more-ordered review of the day's gifts.

Jean may also find that her gratitude for the moment of joyful sharing with her daughter reminds her of other such moments over the years and that she is moved to thank God for the great gift of her daughter throughout her life. Tom may find that his gratitude for the rewarding evening broadens to gratitude for many years of fruitful priestly ministry. Their gratitude will begin with God's gifts given in the time reviewed, but their awareness of those gifts may then expand beyond that time.

However we choose to pray it, step one of the examen will always look *concretely* at the time we are reviewing in order to recognize the specific ways in which God has poured out gifts of love upon us. In deciding how to do this, we are free to follow our hearts' inclinations. Like Jean, we may find it beneficial to discuss our practice with a spiritual guide, a point to which we will return later. Over time the faithful practice of step one will lead each of us to find the way that most helps us to experience God's love through the gifts that love has imparted to us during the day.

We should not hurry past this first step. The first step is not merely a brief moment along the way to what "really matters" in the examen (the subsequent steps). For Ignatius, as we have seen, recognizing God's loving gifts and recognizing God's loving presence through them — summarized in the word "gratitude" — lies at the very heart of our entire relationship with God. The first step focuses on what is primary in our relationship with God, and we do well to give it all the time our hearts desire — without concern for preserving time for the following steps of the examen. In fact, some may find it helpful, for a time or even at length, to focus their examen on step one. Then as they increasingly recognize God's loving presence to them through the gifts each day bestowed upon them, and daily experience how greatly they are loved, the examen as a whole will become more welcome, more sustainable, and more fruitful.[11]

If, like Jean and Tom, we daily endeavor to practice step one of the examen, seeking to review the gifts that a loving God has conferred upon us each day, what will happen? What will we find? Will we recognize such gifts of love in the hours of our own day as well? Ignatius is certain that we will and that once our spiritual eyes are attuned to see we will recognize the inexhaustible abundance of these gifts and of the love they reveal.

The practice of step one, like much else in the life of prayer, normally deepens and grows through faithful exercise over time. If we persevere in praying this step daily, we will find our awareness of God's gifts and of the love that inspires them gradually expanding. We will personally encounter in new and energizing ways that "highest goodness" and that "everlasting love" who desires, as Ignatius tells us, "to give himself to me as much as he can" (*SpirEx*, 234). This is the first blessing that daily examen brings into our lives.

Chapter Four

Second Step: Petition

> *Then he raised his head. "Let us draw God into the world," he cried, "and all need will be quenched."*
> — Martin Buber

"It is all about something that God does"

On one occasion when I took part in a conversation regarding the examen, one person said: "When I make the examen in the evening, I ask the Lord: What do you want to show me about this day? What do you want me to see about this day?" "Because," she said, "it is all about something that God does. It is all about grace." In a few words she had touched the core of what makes the examen effective in our lives. It *is* all about something that God does; it *is* all about grace.

These are not just words. Human effort is indispensable in the practice of examen, but those who undertake it quickly realize that they cannot hope for a faithful and fruitful practice of the examen simply through their own efforts. Their experience teaches them clearly that the insight and transforming power that the examen offers are essentially the work of God's grace within us (1 Cor. 15:10). In the examen, then, after recalling the gifts of God's love (step one) and before reviewing the movements of our hearts and our response to them throughout the day (step three), Ignatius invites us to turn to God in humble prayer, asking for the grace that alone can make our examen fruitful (*SpirEx*, 43). This faith-inspired and hope-filled asking is the second step of the examen; in this step, desire, now warmed by gratitude, takes shape as a *petition* of the heart, asking that vivifying *grace* effect in us what God has inspired us to "wish and desire" (*SpirEx*, 48) as we make the examen each day.

The grace we humbly seek is twofold: the gift of *understanding*, which opens the way to new *freedom*.[1] In this second step we pray for deeper *insight* into God's concrete workings in our day and into any interior movements opposed to those workings, so that we may *act* more surely in overcoming all that hinders our freedom for growth in our relationship with God. As in the preceding chapter, some examples will permit us to explore how this step might be prayed in practice.

Asking for light and strength: A day with Ellen

Ellen is a university student for whom faith in Christ is very real and who desires to grow in her relationship with the Lord. Motivated by this desire, she asked her university chaplain to assist her as spiritual director, and with his help she began the practice of daily examen six months ago. Initially she found it a wonderful means of encountering God in a new way during the day and of increasing her awareness of how she responds to God. Recently, however, the examen has become more difficult, and Ellen is not sure of the reason why. She has discussed this with her director, and she is beginning to realize that something in her both desires and resists the new closeness she is feeling with the Lord. She does not clearly understand this resistance nor does she perceive how she is to progress beyond it.

Ellen usually spends her evenings studying in the library. This is the quietest place and time in her day, and generally she finds this setting conducive for her examen. Upon arriving at the library, she first prays her examen and then begins her evening of study.

THIS EVENING ELLEN SITS IN THE LIBRARY and prays her examen in the usual way. She recognizes God's love in the many gifts given this day, and her heart opens in a response of gratitude for this love. As Ellen now prepares to review the day, she asks the Lord for the light and availability she will need in her examen. She speaks to the Lord of her desire that their mutual love deepen and of her inability to understand and overcome the interior resistance that holds her back. She asks for the gift of spiritual insight into this desire/resistance as she makes her examen. The prayer of the blind man Bartimaeus comes to mind, and she repeats it several times from her heart: "Jesus, Son of David, have mercy on me!" (Mark 10:47). As she prays these words, her heart feels new hope that the Lord will indeed aid her in reviewing her spiritual experience this past day. With a special intensity this evening, Ellen has prayed step two of the examen.

Praying for assistance: A day with Bob

Bob is a married man whose faith was genuine but somewhat marginal in his life for many years. Then a time of difficulty two years ago led him to a renewed interest in Christ; since then he has been growing in his life of faith. When Bob began searching for new ways to grow spiritually, a member of his parish told him about the Ignatian Spiritual Exercises and explained that they can be made in daily life by dedicating an hour each day to prayer and meeting regularly with a spiritual director to discuss the prayer. Bob made the Ignatian retreat in this way and found it an experience of profound grace and growth in his relationship with God. As a fruit of his retreat, he has begun to make the Ignatian examen daily, continuing to meet with his spiritual director for assistance as he does so. Bob has been pleased to find the examen effective in showing him how he can love and serve the Lord more faithfully at home and in the workplace.

Bob's quietest time in the day is his ride on the commuter train to and from work. He generally prays his examen while returning home on the train in the late afternoon.

THIS DAY BOB BEGINS HIS CUSTOMARY EXAMEN as he rides the train after work. He seeks to recognize the Lord's gifts of love during the day but finds this difficult; in fact, he experiences little inclination to make the examen at all. Bob feels tired and his mind continues to dwell on matters of work. The beginnings of his examen have been dry, and Bob is losing hope that the rest of the examen will be any more fruitful. The thought of simply abandoning the examen this afternoon begins to present itself.

When we pray step two of the examen, the difficulties associated with it soften and diminish, and hope wells up within us.

Aware of his inability to pray the examen as he desires, Bob speaks to the Lord, renewing his commitment to the examen and acknowledging his helplessness to pray it with full attention this day. Bob asks the Lord for the assistance he needs to apply himself faithfully to the examen. He humbly prays for the grace of spiritual insight and for the strength to act in accordance with this spiritual insight.

As he makes this prayer, the words of Jesus come to mind: "Whatever you ask in my name, I will do, so that the Father may be glorified in the Son" (John 14:13). Bob makes his prayer for help in Jesus' name, asking that the Father be glorified in the blessing Jesus promises to those who ask in his name. The examen continues to be difficult, but Bob now senses a gentle uplifting of his heart in the midst of the struggle. With a renewed sense of hope, Bob begins to review his interior spiritual experience and his response to it this day. Bob has made step two of the examen with courage and with faith.

Seeking the wisdom of the Spirit: A day with Rita

Rita is a religious woman whose love for God and whose life of service have steadily developed through thirty years of faithful religious life. She has prayed the daily examen for years; it is a prayer that she treasures and faithfully practices, a source of growing sensitivity to God's love and a means of ongoing insight into God's will in the busyness of each day.

RITA HAS COMPLETED her apostolic activity for this day, and her evening meal with the other sisters has just finished. According to her daily practice, she now sits in chapel to pray her evening examen. Her heart is raised in gratitude as she encounters, through the many gifts of the day, the God who shows such continuing love for her. Rita then turns her heart to the Holy Spirit, seeking the light and strength that will make her examen this evening a grace-filled time of spiritual growth. She humbly opens her human desire and human limitation to the Spirit's power and love, asking for the gift of spiritual wisdom to discern the things of the Spirit in her examen: which stirrings this day have been of God and which have not, whether she was aware of these and how she responded to them. She asks the Spirit to be a living fountain of truth and strength within her as she examines the day. With a trusting heart, Rita now begins to consider her spiritual experience throughout this day. Raising her heart to the Spirit in a way long habitual for her, Rita has prayed step two of the examen.

The practice of step two: Petition

The fruitfulness of the daily examen hinges upon several supporting dispositions, themselves the work of grace. Examen is born of a fire of longing to grow in the love of the Lord, is nourished by the courage to seek moral and spiritual transformation day by day in our lives, and fosters spiritual growth when practiced with patient daily fidelity. Examen entails attentive consideration both of the spiritual movements stirring daily in our hearts and of our response to them; it involves, therefore, exploring spiritual realities that our human poverty alone cannot hope to grasp (1 Cor. 2:9–13).

The practice of step two simply transforms into prayer what all who love the Lord already know: Who of us can hope to pray the examen perseveringly and insightfully if unaided (John 15:5)? Who of us can hope for that fruitful daily practice of the examen that our hearts desire if unassisted by the Spirit's wisdom and love?

Such questions clearly manifest the great need for and the power in this second step of the examen. The practice of step two infuses the examen with a warm and rich sense of hope. This heartfelt and trust-filled petition opens our poverty to the One who is rich, and whose richness lovingly and superabundantly provides for our poverty. Though assistance is available to us in various ways should we struggle with the examen, here in step two Ignatius has nonetheless already provided the most fundamental solution to all such difficulties: that we humbly and sincerely *ask* for that outpouring of God's grace and love that enables us to do all things (Phil. 4:13) and so empowers us to practice the examen as a truly transforming prayer.

Step two also solidly situates the examen in its single, necessary spiritual space: a space of *prayer,* of *grace,* of *gift,* of *God's loving action* in our lives. When we pray step two of the examen, the difficulties associated with it soften and diminish, and hope wells up within us. Experience of the examen so prayed will teach us that that hope will not be disappointed.

In step two, Ignatius simply invites us to ask for light and strength without specifying further the manner in which this petition is to be made. How we choose concretely to make the petition of step two will be our individual decision, according to what we personally find most helpful. At times, as in the examples of Ellen and Bob, we will sense a particular need for step two and may spend longer on it than on other days. At other times, as with Rita, it will be a peaceful and hope-filled moment as we move toward step three in the examen. Ongoing practice of the examen will lead us, like Ellen, Bob, and Rita, to find our own way to pray step two, a way that, like much in the life of prayer, may vary and evolve over time. In this way, blessed by gratitude and strengthened by petition, we will be richly prepared for continuing growth in the prayer of examen.

Chapter Five

Third Step: Review

Do not run or fly away in order to become free. Rather, go deeply into the narrow space given you. There you will find God and all things.
— Gustave Thibon

What Ignatius reviews

In step three, Ignatius says, we consider the day we are reviewing "hour by hour, or from one period of time to another" (*SpirEx*, 43). For what, within the total richness of our interior experience, are we looking? What is the *content* of this spiritual review?

We may answer this question by asking another: For what was Ignatius looking when he reviewed his own interior experience on March 12, 1544? What kinds of experience did he note as spiritually significant? A brief return to Ignatius's journal for that day will assist us in replying. Having observed Ignatius's own experience of such a review, we may then consider what form our own review in step three might assume.

Ignatius begins his journal for March 12 by remembering his morning prayer and the stirrings he sensed within it: "I felt much devotion, and from the midpoint on, there was much of it, clear, lucid, and, as it were, warm" (380).[1] Ignatius is attentive to what occurs during his prayer and notes the unfolding of the experience in its beginning, its midpoint, and through to its conclusion. He perceives the affective quality of his prayer as it

75

develops: the warmth and *spiritual consolation*[2] he feels in the Lord, accompanied by a sense of *clarity* and light.

Ignatius's review includes the Mass as well and his spiritual experience as he prepares for and then celebrates it. A sense of spiritual consolation continues during a part of the Mass, and Ignatius feels "much devotion and at times movements toward tears" (380). Both before the Mass and during it, however, Ignatius notes a certain trouble in his heart: "I did not feel prepared.... I struggled repeatedly ... " (380). He is also able to name the cause of this interior trouble: "since I was not finding what I was seeking" (380).

After the Mass Ignatius undergoes an experience of *spiritual desolation*.[3] In his journal he notes both the *affective* quality of this desolation and the *thoughts* that arise from it (*SpirEx*, 317, 318). Ignatius *feels* "remote" and "separated" from the Persons of the Trinity, and he perceives that this feeling casts an affective shadow over both past and future: "as if I had never felt their presence and never would again" (381). As he experiences these troubling spiritual feelings, Ignatius also finds himself "confused with various *thoughts*" arising from his feelings (381). He is attentive to these thoughts and notes them: the thought of distancing himself from the community in order to find the quiet he desires, the thought of fasting, the thought of rejecting an already clear decision and beginning anew the process of deciding, and, finally, the thought of moving the chapel to a quieter place (381). Aware that he is experiencing spiritual desolation, Ignatius chooses not to follow the suggestions of his confusing thoughts (*SpirEx*, 318).

He decides rather to explore the *cause* of his spiritual desolation (*SpirEx*, 319), and he finds it in his desire that God conform to his own perception of how the decision regarding poverty should conclude: "I was seeking to look for too many signs and ... I wanted them given within a period of time or in the celebration of Masses which would end according to my satisfaction" (381). With new clarity — the fruit of his attentive review of his desire — Ignatius now chooses to *act* accordingly: "Once I recognized that I felt this inclination and that this was different from what God desired, I began to note this and to strive to move my heart toward what was pleasing to God" (382).

In his journal, Ignatius then describes how, in seeking to conform his heart to God's desire, "the darkness gradually began to lift and tears to come" (382). Having grasped the cause of his spiritual desolation and having striven to overcome it (*SpirEx,* 319), Ignatius finds that his spiritual desolation does indeed disappear and that spiritual consolation returns to him. He finds further that in this warm time of spiritual consolation he experiences a complete harmonization of his will with God's will: "I felt all desire to say more Masses for this purpose disappear" (382) — Ignatius has completely embraced God's will and no further search is necessary.

Because Ignatius has attended to and understood his spiritual experience so clearly, when various thoughts now arise counseling him to delay or to reconsider his decision regarding poverty, he quickly rejects them, identifying them as of "the bad spirit" (382) or, as he frequently writes, of "the enemy."[4] Thus Ignatius notes and firmly refuses the suggestion of celebrating further Masses under pretext of giving thanks to God, thereby prolonging the already-concluded process of discernment (382). He likewise rejects a subsequent thought urging him to wait until evening to conclude the process, knowing clearly that the time to act is already upon him; as he considers this thought, Ignatius notes in himself a diminishment of spiritual consolation, a further confirmation that such delay would not be of God (382). Finally, during his midday meal, Ignatius senses the first faint stirrings of doubt regarding his decision and simply dismisses them as not of God (383). In this way, Ignatius's spiritual struggles of March 12 conclude in peace of heart and with clarity.

We may return now to our earlier question: For what was Ignatius looking when he reviewed his own interior experience on March 12, 1544? What kinds of experience did he note as spiritually significant?

Ignatius is attentive to distinguish the *spiritual consolations* and *spiritual desolations* he experiences as his busy day unfolds: in prayer, in preparing for Mass, during Mass, in his place of work, and during a meal. He notices the *thoughts* that arise from these consolations and desolations, whether the grace-inspired insight that accompanies spiritual consolation or the confusing thoughts born of spiritual desolation. He is careful to discern which thoughts are of *God* and which are of the *enemy,* and so to *accept* those that are of God and *reject* those that are of the enemy. Ignatius strives to understand the spiritual *desires* of his own heart and to discern whether these are in accord with God's desire or not. When he recognizes that his desire is not in harmony with God's, Ignatius actively seeks to conform his desire to God's desire.

Ignatius's sensitive and ongoing attention to his interior spiritual experience throughout the day results in an ability to identify clearly what in his experience is of God and what is not. This clarity in turn enhances his capacity to choose and to act in the day with spiritual wisdom. Ignatius's attentive and discerning review of his spiritual experience leads him to spiritual freedom: freedom from deception and freedom to say "yes" this day, with all the unified energy of his being, to the God he loves.

What we review

Spiritual consolation and spiritual desolation — times of energizing joy in the Lord and times of interior heaviness in our life of faith — are the common experience of us all. How aware of these are we when our hearts experience them? And how do we respond to them? Thoughts arise in all of us, both God-inspired thoughts that offer clarity for spiritually fruitful action and confusing thoughts inspired by the enemy (from the tempter, from within the self, from our surroundings), which, if unreflectively followed, will lead to spiritual harm. Again, how aware of such thoughts are we? Can we discern which are of God and should be followed, and which are not and should be rejected?

Like Ignatius, we may have expectations of the way God will act in our lives, which may occasion interior struggles when events prove, in fact, different from our expectations. When such struggles occur, how conscious are we of their cause? How quickly are we aware of that cause? Are we able, like Ignatius, to strive to harmonize the desires of our hearts with the desires of God's heart for us, and so progress toward the peace that flows from communion of heart with God?

Each of our days is filled with a richness of interior experience: love, hopes, anxieties, joys, fears, attractions, resistances, desires, disinclinations, all accompanied by an endless flux of varied thoughts. This interior experience occurs in the context of continual and constantly changing activity: interactions with others, conversations, meals, prayer, work, travel, projects, planning, and decision-making. In the prayer of examen we ask: Where was God in all of this today? Toward what was the Lord calling me in the day? How did I respond to this call? Were there inclinations and thoughts this day that were not of God? If there were, was I able to discern and resist them? Was the use of my freedom in accord with God's loving desire for me today?

Ignatius's experience is his own, and it is furthermore the experience of one long accustomed to a discerning awareness of personal spiritual experience. Further examples will serve to expand our vision of how step three might appear in the concrete reality of daily spiritual living today. These examples will situate the examen in some of the widely diverse spiritual contexts of individual lives.

A walk with the Lord: A day with Don

Don is a fourth-year university student whose faith had been of little importance to him until several months ago. In his first three

years at the university he had abandoned Sunday Mass and had
essentially ceased to consider religious matters. In various ways
Don had adopted the lifestyle of his surroundings, vaguely aware
that this was not in accord with his nominal faith.

Still, something felt too empty in his life, and when another
student invited him to a talk at the university chapel one evening,
somewhat to his own surprise Don accepted the invitation. He
liked the talk and found the sharing among the students afterward
welcome. Don attended several such evenings and eventually re-
sumed participation in Sunday Mass with the student group of
which by now he was a part. A few months ago Don took part
in a weekend retreat for young adults. The retreat made a great
impression on Don; he wanted in his own life more of the peace
and sense of meaning that he saw in others on the retreat. He
knew that he desired the deeper relationship with the Lord Jesus
that these others seemed to possess.

> Like Ignatius, we may have expectations
> of the way God will act in our lives,
> which may occasion interior struggles
> when events prove, in fact, different from
> our expectations.

Don spoke with the retreat director and shared all that was
stirring in his heart. He told the director that he wanted to grow
closer to Christ, that he knew he needed to change the way he
was living, and that he was willing to try though he did not see
clearly what he should do. As they spoke Don mentioned his habit
of taking a walk in the evenings when possible. He explained
that he enjoyed the physical movement after a day of study and
that he always found nature uplifting. Such walks, he said, were
often the only quiet space in his day. The director suggested that
Don try taking his evening walk with the Lord Jesus and that

with the Lord he review his day, open to what the Lord might show him about it. The director also invited Don, if he wished, to return after a few weeks and discuss his experience of these walks. Don liked the idea and began the practice of reviewing his day in this way.

As DON IS WALKING THIS EVENING, he is aware that something is troubling him. He asks the Lord to help him understand why he feels so unsettled this day. Don recognizes that he has felt somewhat burdened throughout the entire afternoon. Now he remembers when this feeling first began. He was walking to class after lunch and encountered a woman student of his same year in the university. They had been friends and had shared quite deeply in the past but had not seen each other in recent weeks. Don was completely unprepared for the intense anger she showed toward him and for the cutting remarks she made. When Don became angry in turn and replied in kind, she simply walked away. Since that moment he has felt no peace.

Don now asks the Lord to be with him and to help him understand what has happened. He thinks back to the last time he saw his classmate. He remembers that this was at a party and that he and his friends had been drinking heavily. When Don saw his classmate nearby, he repeated to the group some profoundly personal things she had shared in one of their conversations. At the time, together with his friends and under the influence of alcohol, it seemed humorous, and Don thought no more about it until today. Now he perceives how painfully embarrassing that moment must have been for this woman and how deeply betrayed she must have felt.

As he continues walking Don realizes with a sense of shame (*SpirEx,* 314) that he has treated this woman very badly. He sees that he will need to apologize to her, that he must do what he can to repair the harm he has done to her, and that he must seek if at all possible to restore the trust that he has betrayed. Don also recognizes that he needs to examine his drinking habits.

Suddenly he begins to wonder whether under the influence of alcohol he may also have hurt others in ways that he failed to grasp at the time. He plans to explore this too with the Lord in a future evening review.

As he completes his walk, Don quietly thanks the Lord for the insight he has been given. He decides that he will speak with the retreat director about what he has seen this evening and will ask his help toward effectively making these changes in his life.

In Ignatian terms, Don has experienced the third step of the examen in a profoundly fruitful way. He has examined a troubling movement of his heart with courage and sincerity. The resulting insight clearly has great potential for moral and spiritual growth in Don's life: in the way he relates to women and to friends in general, and with respect to alcohol and its abuse. His examen further leads to the spiritually beneficial decision to speak with the retreat director a second time.

What is different in Don's life because he is making the examen? What might happen if he were not? What will change in his life of faith if Don perseveres in his evening walk with the Lord throughout his final year in college? If he continues this practice after college and in the years to come?

An experience of discernment:
A day with Susan

Susan is a single professional woman in her early thirties. She and the man she is dating are both aware that they will soon be engaged. Susan loves the Lord and since her early twenties has lived a profound life of faith and prayer. Five years ago she began spiritual direction and, soon after, the director suggested that she undertake the practice of examen. Susan was intrigued by his explanation of the examen and began to pray it daily. Over the past five years she has made it faithfully, seldom omitting it as part of her daily spiritual life. In conversation with her spiritual director three months ago, Susan decided to attend daily Mass when possible. She found a church with morning Mass at an hour that allowed her ample time to get to work. Since then Susan has made her examen in church after the morning Mass. She treasures this time of reviewing the preceding day with the Lord and of preparing spiritually for the day about to begin.

TODAY SUSAN SITS IN CHURCH after Mass, embraced by the Lord's love and Eucharistic presence. She is aware of a serene sense of interior well-being and God's love is very real for her at this moment (*SpirEx*, 316). As she considers the spiritual consolation she is feeling, Susan realizes that since she began attending weekday Mass she experiences God's peace more frequently than before and that she has more patience and greater availability to others during the workday. She is grateful for the grace at work in her and is confirmed in the rightness of her decision to attend daily Mass when possible.

Now Susan looks back over the preceding day. She remembers that the day did not begin well. God had seemed far away and she had felt little energy for spiritual things (*SpirEx*, 317). Susan recalls how she almost decided to omit the morning Mass as planned; finally she did go, though she arrived late for the Mass. She recognizes that her near omission of Mass was not due to physical indisposition or to any concrete external obstacle, but rather to her heaviness of heart upon rising. Now she identifies that heaviness and that sense that God was so distant as spiritual desolation. Susan recognizes here the enemy's tactic of urging us to change our spiritual proposals in time of spiritual desolation (*SpirEx*, 318) and thanks God for the grace that enabled her — not without struggle — to maintain her proposal of attending Mass as planned. She resolves to watch for similar deceptions of the enemy in the future and to resist them firmly in their beginnings (*SpirEx*, 325).

Susan also remembers arriving at work that morning and seeing a fellow worker who is facing serious personal problems. Susan had planned to share the lunch hour with the woman that day, knowing that the other would appreciate the chance to talk. Still feeling spiritually dry, however, and with little desire to listen to another's burdens, Susan decided to wait for another day and did not approach the other woman during the lunch hour. Susan now sees what she did not in the moment yesterday: that spiritual desolation had led her to postpone a gesture of love already planned for that day. Susan thanks the Lord for the insight of her examen this morning, asks the Lord's forgiveness for her delay in showing love, and resolves to invite her coworker to lunch today. Susan leaves the church grateful for the blessing of her examen and spiritually ready to begin her day.

The third step of the examen has greatly assisted Susan this morning. The growth in God's peace (spiritual consolation) as a result of attending weekday Mass confirms her in that practice as willed by the Lord. Because of the morning's insight, Susan will adhere to this practice all the more firmly in the future. The examen has fortified her commitment to a channel of grace rich in possibilities of further progress in the Spirit.

Because she identified the spiritual desolation that she had not noticed the day before and recognized how it had urged her to change her spiritual plans (to attend Mass that morning, to show love to a person in need at work), Susan could now evaluate clearly her spiritual decisions of that day and, as a result, will have greater freedom to make sound spiritual decisions in the future. If she feels a similar sense of spiritual desolation before Mass again, Susan will now more probably notice and identify it for the spiritual desolation that it is.[5] She is consequently more likely to remain faithfully committed to attending Mass each day. After her examen this day, Susan is also less likely to delay an act of love should spiritual desolation again suggest such delay.

As above with Don, we may once more ask here: What is different in Susan's life because she is making the examen? Because she made the examen this day? What might have happened if she had not? Already her years of faithfully praying the examen have developed in Susan a growing spiritual sensitivity. With the help of her examen, she is able to recognize spiritual consolation and spiritual desolation, and to respond effectively to both. How might this spiritual sensitivity develop further if Susan continues to pray the examen in the years to come? Susan does not possess the highly refined spiritual sensitivity that Ignatius manifests in his *Spiritual Diary*, but her spiritual awareness has already grown, and, if she perseveres in the examen, will continue to grow. The blessings of such discerning awareness in the spiritual life are evident.

The practice of step three: Review

The settings that different persons choose for this review vary widely. They may choose a quiet moment with morning coffee, a ride on a commuter train, a walk outdoors, a church and the Eucharistic presence of the Lord, or any other setting that provides a favorable opportunity for this prayerful review. The Ignatian principle regarding prayer in general also applies here: reflection on our experience of prayer — here the examen — will teach us which settings best assist us to gain the fruit we seek in the prayer (*SpirEx*, 77). A holy creativity will lead us to discover what those circumstances may be with respect to the examen.

Ignatius also suggests that we review the day "hour by hour, or from one period of time to another": the times we spent in prayer, with family, or community; the principal moments of our activity in the day; the sharing at meals; and the times of relaxation. In this review we look for the spiritual consolations that the Lord may have given during the day, noting where the Lord may be leading us through them (Ignatius is confirmed in his decision to end the process of discernment; Susan is confirmed in her decision to attend weekday Mass).[6] We also attend to any spiritual desolation that may have been present and note our response to it: Did we resist it firmly? Did we allow it to change our spiritual proposals (such as Susan and the office worker)? Do we feel it still? If so, how might we actively and effectively resist it (*SpirEx*, 313–27)?

Simultaneously we watch for possible invitations from the Lord to moral growth (Don and the woman student, his use of alcohol, Susan's readiness to assist her coworker), thus progressing in freedom to love the God by whom we know ourselves so loved.[7]

Step three, prayed faithfully and in the way best suited to each person, contains enormous potential for growth in our capacity to notice, understand, and respond fruitfully to the spiritual movements of our hearts, and so to increase in Gospel love. This is yet another powerful spiritual gift the examen offers us.

Chapter Six

Fourth Step: Forgiveness

*I raised my head. "Let ourselves go, like a
child — is that all?" He nodded his head,
agreeing. I said nothing more . . . invaded by
a sudden joy.*   — Matthew Silvan

Forgiveness and relationship

The fourth step, Ignatius says, is "to ask forgiveness of God our
Lord for my failings" (*SpirEx*, 43). This step in which we ask for
and receive God's *forgiveness* touches deep relational spaces in
our hearts. We must approach it with great sensitivity, for much
in the practice of examen depends upon how we understand and
what our hearts feel in regard to this: asking God's forgiveness.

Jean Vanier writes: "Forgiveness and celebration are at the
heart of community."[1] The two pillars that sustain relationships are the joy of togetherness and the readiness, when human
limitation emerges, to ask forgiveness. Vanier continues:

> We can only truly accept others as they are, and forgive
> them, when we discover that we are truly accepted by God as
> we are and forgiven by him. It is a deep experience, knowing
> that we are loved and held by God in all our brokenness and
> littleness.[2]

In its fourth step, the examen is the privileged daily space of
this "deep experience" of "knowing that we are loved and held
by God in all our brokenness and littleness." To live the fourth
step daily in all its richness strengthens our communion with

87

God and empowers us to be agents of healing forgiveness in our communities, in our families, and in society as a whole.

At this point the wisdom of the order in the steps of the examen emerges. Within the examen much has preceded and prepared us for the fourth step; this context is key to praying the fourth step as Ignatius intends it. For Ignatius, God's love is *always* the first consideration, and all else is viewed after and only in the light of this love.[3] The first step in the examen, and the basis for all that follows, is simply to notice the endless outpouring of God's gifts of love to us in the day. When the human heart knows that another heart loves it deeply, faithfully, and unconditionally, it loses all fear. It may ask with trust for any forgiveness it seeks because it *already knows that it is unshakably loved.* The prayer of step one (gratitude) is uniquely powerful in preparing space in our hearts for the prayer of step four (forgiveness).

Our image of God

Do our hearts truly know that God loves us unshakably? Can we readily ask God's forgiveness or do we hesitate before this request? Is the fourth step welcome to us or does something within us feel uneasy when we sense that we need God's forgiveness?

> The God of Christian revelation is a God who rejoices in the encounter of forgiveness, whose loving forgiveness respects human dignity and heals human hurt.

To be human is to be wonderfully gifted by the Creator but also unavoidably entails limitation on various levels of our being. Such limitation will appear in different ways as we review our experience daily in the third step of the examen. How do we relate to God when these limitations surface? How does Don relate to God when he sees that he has hurt another person? How does Susan relate to God when she realizes that she has delayed an act of love to a fellow worker? Do Don and Susan know that they are loved and held by God in all their brokenness and littleness? Do we know that we are loved and held by God in all our brokenness and littleness?

I have never forgotten a conversation about the examen one day with a group of religious men. One man said: "For twenty years I made the examen every night. And every night, for twenty years, I came up short. Finally I realized that God is not like this." Clearly this man had good will to make the examen. Equally clearly he was faithful to the practice of the examen for many years. Yet the examen was for him a persistent source of heaviness: "And every night, for twenty years, I came up short." His concluding words "Finally I realized that God is not like this" indicate one reason why we may shy away from the examen or may find it daunting in some measure when we pray it. Much in the practice of examen depends on our sense, as this man says, of "what God is like" or in more formal language, on our *image* of the God who is our relational "Other" in the prayer of examen.[4]

When this man realized "that God is not like this" he was right. The God of Christian revelation is a God who rejoices in the encounter of forgiveness, whose loving forgiveness respects human dignity and heals human hurt. Joy is nowhere so repeatedly mentioned in the Gospels as in Luke 15, the chapter of the parables of forgiveness: the lost sheep, the lost coin, and the prodigal son. The profound link in the Scriptures between God's forgiveness and joy indicates that the more truly we experience step four of the examen, the more this step will become a time of *joy*.

"Love bade me welcome"

Do we find it so now? Growth in the prayer of the fourth step of the examen entails growth in *this* image of God both in our *thinking* about God and in our *affective* response to God. This growth may occur in different ways and over varying lengths of time for each one of us. The process of such growth is beautifully articulated in George Herbert's poem "Love."[5] An ongoing dialogue between human hesitation and God's warm and insistent invitation leads, by stages, to communion. We may note as we read this poem that the narrator, from the perspective of the present, is attentively reviewing past spiritual experience — a striking illustration of the prayer of examen. Herbert describes this spiritual journey:

> Love bade me welcome: yet my soul drew back,
>   Guilty of dust and sin.
> But quick-eyed Love, observing me grow slack[6]
>   From my first entrance in,
> Drew nearer to me, sweetly questioning
>   If I lacked anything.[7]
>
> "A guest," I answered, "worthy to be here";
>   Love said, "You shall be he."
> "I, the unkind, ungrateful? Ah, my dear,
>   I cannot look on thee."
> Love took my hand, and smiling did reply,
>   "Who made the eyes but I?"
>
> "Truth, Lord; but I have marred them; let my shame
>   Go where it doth deserve."
> "And know you not," says Love, "who bore the blame?"
>   "My dear, then I will serve."
> "You must sit down," says Love, "and taste my meat."
>   "So I did sit and eat."

The movement through successive stages from the first exchange in this divine-human dialogue, "Love bade me welcome: *yet my soul drew back,* / Guilty of dust and sin," to the final sharing, "So I did sit and eat," describes the growth that renders step four of the examen progressively more welcome and joy-filled. If our souls should in fact "draw back" when we consider the practice of examen, one reason for this disinclination and the tiredness or struggle to find time that may express it, may be our image of "what God is like." When we fully encounter the God revealed by Jesus Christ and know "that we are loved and held by God in all our brokenness and littleness," then much may change in how we *feel* about the examen and consequently in how we pray it. Growth in our image of God is a significant factor in a growing practice of the examen itself.[8]

In his *Spiritual Diary* for April 2, 1544, Ignatius considers "the time of my faults."[9] These are the times, he says, in which he does not receive God's spiritual visitation because of "not having disposed myself or helped myself throughout the day, or in giving place to some thoughts that distracted me from his words in the sacrifice [the Mass] and from his divine majesty" (390–91). Ignatius recognizes that even in the times of such — to us — slight faults, it is better for him not to experience spiritual consolation since this absence alerts him to his failings and permits him to address them so that he might live uninterruptedly in the presence of the God he loves, as his heart so desires.

And Ignatius perceives "that God our Lord orders this (who loves me more than I love myself), for my greater spiritual benefit" (391). "Who loves me more than I love myself": beautiful words, and words that strikingly reveal Ignatius's image of God. The God he knows is a God who always, even "in the time of my faults," "loves me more than I love myself." With such an image of God in his heart, Ignatius views his faults peacefully, brings them to God with trust, and, as he does so, finds renewed strength in God's love. This is the portrait of the fourth step of the examen in all its power for spiritual growth.

The practice of step four: Forgiveness

Like step two, step four consists in *asking* ("to ask forgiveness of God our Lord"), a petition that underlines once again the nature of examen as *grace* and as a gift to be humbly sought of God.[10] And we ask this of the God who promises that what we ask for in prayer we will receive (Matt. 7:7).

Reflection on such petitioning leads directly to the core reality of step four. In his text (*SpirEx*, 43) Ignatius is outlining a "spiritual *exercise*"; he describes what *we* do in praying step four of the examen: *we* ask forgiveness of God our Lord. This is our part in step four, and it is key to the prayer of examen. Such petitioning is nonetheless simply the gateway to the more important reality of step four, and that is what *God* does in response to our request: the loving embrace, the welcoming kiss, the joyful celebration, and the outpouring of new life that we call forgiveness (Luke 15:20–23). Step four liberates, transforms, and joyfully energizes us when in praying it we move spiritually from *our* asking for forgiveness to an awareness of *God's* response, as Jesus reveals it, to our petitioning. Said another way, step four is an exquisitely *Christian* exercise, a means of experiencing in the concrete reality of each day the foundational truth of all Christianity: that "God so loved the world that he gave his only Son" that we might have life, and that "God did not send his Son into the world to condemn the world, but that the world might be saved through him" (John 3:16–17).

It follows, therefore, that step four, like all of the examen, is an essentially *relational* step, the human person in relationship with the divine Person; we ask forgiveness "*of God* our Lord." The examen is not the self-evaluation of a heart in isolation but rather a colloquy (*SpirEx*, 53, 61), a conversation, a dialogue between two hearts. This point, which perhaps seems obvious when stated in writing, may be not at all obvious in practice and cannot be emphasized too much. It is in turning to the God who "is greater than our hearts" (1 John 3:20) that our hearts are set free from self-accusation and that a spiritual road to growth in love opens before us. When we pray the examen (and when we discuss this prayer with a spiritual guide), we will find it beneficial to explore in what measure and in what way we experience step four as *relational*.

We said at the beginning of our reflections on the examen that this entire prayer is rooted in *desire*. Those who love deeply desire, like Ignatius, that nothing even minimally diminish the fullness of their communion with the Triune God they love. Out of this desire for communion in love the *desire for forgiveness* is born. When we experience day after day how this forgiveness in which "we are loved and held by God in all our brokenness and littleness" infuses new vitality into our communion with God, then the grace of step four is at work within us. Step four has become the joyful encounter with God that Ignatius, in keeping with all of Christian revelation, understands forgiveness to be.

Step four is an essentially *relational* step, the human person in relationship with the divine Person.

For what do we ask forgiveness? From this perspective, step four follows naturally upon step three. Don will ask forgiveness for the way that he has failed to respect the woman student; Susan will ask forgiveness for her delay, caused by spiritual desolation, in showing concern for a fellow worker; Ignatius will ask forgiveness for "not having disposed myself or helped myself throughout the day" to remain in communion with the Lord. As we pray the review of step three, we may notice times when we have allowed the message of spiritual consolation to slip from our consciousness, have surrendered in varying measure to the heaviness and suggestions of spiritual desolation, or have not lived Jesus' new commandment of love to the full measure our hearts desire. If we recognize such times as we review the day, then we stand on the spiritually rich threshold of step four: the healing encounter between human need and divine love that takes place in Jesus

Christ. Through step four this blessed encounter becomes real in the day we are living.

In describing step four Ignatius simply states that we "ask forgiveness of God our Lord." As with earlier steps in the examen, he does not specify how we do this. All who practice the examen will find their personal way to pray the asking-receiving of step four. We may choose to ask freely from our hearts. We may find inspiration in appropriate words of Scripture, in contemplation of an icon, in the Eucharistic presence of the Lord — in any way that is according to what our hearts desire and what we find helpful. Ignatius's principle of freedom in exploring options, reflecting on our experience, and choosing what that experience reveals to be most efficacious (*SpirEx,* 77) applies to the practice of step four in the examen. Then our examen and our spiritual lives will be blessed with the gift of forgiveness sought and received.

Chapter Seven

Fifth Step: Renewal

It is like a kind of awakening, a sort of intimation of all that may happen the day after tomorrow — what tremendous possibilities!
— Thomas Merton

Looking to the future

When we contemplate Ignatius's review of his spiritual experience on March 12, 1544, we discover a constant pattern: Ignatius looks *back* in order to look *forward*. Through noting what he has experienced earlier in the day, Ignatius gains clarity for the spiritual choices that lie ahead.

Thus when Ignatius examines his spiritual desolation after the Mass on that day and realizes that he "was seeking to look for too many signs" and that he "wanted them given within a period of time or in the celebration of Masses which would end according to my satisfaction" (381),[1] he perceives the direction his heart must take: "Once I recognized that I felt this inclination and that this was different from what God desired, I began to note this and to strive to move my heart toward what was pleasing to God" (382). An insightful review of his preceding experience permits Ignatius to choose wisely the spiritual path the Lord desires as the day continues to unfold. As we have seen, Ignatius notes that "with this the darkness gradually began to lift and tears began to come" (382).

Later in the same day new thoughts arise in Ignatius's mind: to add more Masses to the decision-making process in order to

95

give thanks, to delay the ending of the decision-making process until evening, and to doubt yet again his decision to end this process of discernment. Because, however, he has reviewed his earlier spiritual experience and found clarity in his decision to end the process, Ignatius is able to act decisively in each case. He rejects each suggestion as it arises and remains unswervingly faithful to the light he has received (382–83). His discernment remains intact and his heart is confirmed in peace (383).

If, then, Ignatius considers his *past* spiritual experience, he does so with the *future* in mind. This same principle underlies the entire practice of the examen as Ignatius outlines it for us.

> The examen in its fifth step is the prayer of *spiritual progress.*

In steps one through four, those praying the examen have looked *back* from the perspective of the present (this evening, for example) over the spiritual experience of the preceding hours. In so doing they have perceived more profoundly God's love at work in their day and have noted their own response to that love as the day has progressed. Now in the fifth step, their examen looks *ahead* to the day to come and projects the light of the preceding steps onto that time. The fifth step, Ignatius writes, is "to propose amendment with God's grace."[2]

This final step adds a further dimension to the already-rich prayer of the examen. Thus far the examen has illuminated the past day. Now the examen becomes the cutting edge of spiritual growth for the day to follow. The examen in its fifth step is the prayer of *spiritual progress.*

As we look to the coming day, we normally have a general sense of what that day is likely to hold. We know, broadly speaking, where we will be, with whom we will be, and how we will be occupied. From the preceding steps in the examen, we already possess a concrete awareness of how God's love is calling us to grow. In the fifth step we focus that concrete awareness on the next day as we foresee it and plan specifically how we will respond to God's call to growth: "with this person the gift of patience will be needed; in this place, perseverance; in this occupation, the gift of self-control if someone or some group of people is not to be denied justice; and so forth."[3] In this way, like Ignatius, we are constantly learning from our experience, and that experience becomes a resource for continual spiritual growth. Some examples will illustrate how this may occur in practice.

Spiritual growth: A day with Joan

Joan is a married woman with three young children. She is a woman of faith and active in her parish. Her marriage is strong. Joan carries two principal concerns in her heart. One of her children is struggling in school, and Joan and her husband are unsure of how to assist their child in his difficulties. In addition, her husband's company is planning to downsize soon and his job is in jeopardy.

A few months ago a friend gave Joan a copy of a monthly publication providing a brief meditation on the Scripture readings for the Mass of the day. Joan liked it and subscribes to it now. She reads it when she is able and finds it helpful. This morning Joan read the meditation for the day. The Gospel was the multiplication of the loaves and fish (Matt. 14:13–21), and Joan found the meditation comforting: Christ provides for his people in their need.

IN THE AFTERNOON Joan drives to school to meet her children and bring them home. She arrives a little early. As she waits in the car Joan finds herself reflecting on her concerns for her husband and her child. She also remembers her reading of the meditation on the Gospel this morning. Joan realizes that the reading has given her greater peace in facing her cares this day. Her heart lifts up in gratitude to the Lord for the gift of that daily reading and for this brief time of prayer in the afternoon.

Joan finds this short moment of reflection helpful and wonders how she may continue to pray in this way during the day. She considers that similar moments of waiting, though brief, do occur throughout the day and might serve for reflection in this same way. Joan decides to watch for such moments and in them to share her day with the Lord Jesus, seeking his strength and his light. When her children approach Joan greets them warmly, with renewed peace in her heart.

In a simple and effective way, Joan has prayed step five of the examen. She has looked *back* over her spiritual experience of the day, and through this review she has observed what may be spiritually helpful for the *future*. As a fruit of this review Joan understands more deeply the value of her brief daily meditation and will also begin to watch for moments that may permit a short prayer of examen. If Joan continues this practice of prayerful review in the days to come, we may hope with good reason that further spiritual fruit will follow.

Choosing commitments:
A day with Kevin

Kevin is a deacon in his final year of seminary studies. He loves the Lord and sincerely seeks spiritual growth. Kevin does well in his classes and is a leader among his peers. Because he is so capable Kevin is often asked to assist in activities in the seminary and in the parish to which he is assigned as deacon. He finds these activities uplifting and willingly accepts these requests.

KEVIN GENERALLY MAKES HIS EXAMEN during his customary time of prayer before supper. As he prays the examen today Kevin notes that recently his studies and his relationships with his fellow seminarians have been more difficult than usual. He knows that he is overly tired and that consequently everything requires more effort and is less enjoyable than before. Kevin realizes that the many activities he has accepted, though good in themselves, are difficult to sustain together with his studies and daily seminary life. He now questions the wisdom of having said "yes" so readily to so many requests. Kevin decides to discuss this with his spiritual director and to explore what changes may be necessary in choosing his commitments.

Kevin too has practiced step five of the examen with spiritual profit. He has looked *back* over his recent experience and understood that with good intentions he has overextended his physical and emotional energies. Kevin recognizes the harm that may occur should the present pattern continue in the future. His decision to speak with his spiritual director is wise (*SpirEx,* 326) and will most likely lead to sound decisions in the days that lie *ahead.*

In the midst of turmoil: A day with Elaine

Elaine is a woman religious in her fifties who serves in the diocesan office for evangelization. She is a woman of faithful prayer, esteemed within her community, and sensitive to the needs of others around her. Each day she walks to the office and returns home on public transportation. Three years ago, when Elaine began to work in the office for evangelization, she found that the morning walk and evening bus ride provided welcome space for a reflective sharing with the Lord about the day. Since that time she has maintained this practice regularly. These two times of reflection help Elaine to be more aware of the Lord's love throughout her day and have become an important part of her prayer.

Three days ago, Elaine went to the doctor for her regular checkup. She had always enjoyed good health and so was totally unprepared when the doctor found a growth that was possibly cancerous. In reply to the doctor's question, Elaine told him that there is in fact a history of cancer in her family. The doctor explained that Elaine would need an operation soon and they discussed a date. He could not assure her that the growth was benign.

THE FOLLOWING DAY ELAINE walked to her office as usual. She was overwhelmed by the seriousness and the unexpectedness of what had happened. Elaine admitted to herself that she was afraid. As she walked she poured out her confusion and fear to the Lord. The busyness of the day then intervened. When she returned home on the bus that afternoon, Elaine again opened her heart to the Lord, still afraid and still unable to grasp the meaning of her suddenly changed condition.

The next day on her way to and from work, Elaine again shared with the Lord all that was stirring in her heart. The confusion and fear remained, but began to feel less totally overwhelming. Somehow she knew that God's love was with her and would accompany her in the weeks ahead.

Today Elaine walks to work once more, reviewing with the Lord all that has happened and all that her heart feels. She is aware of more peace, though the fear has not disappeared, and she realizes that this peace is not simply due to the passage of a few days. In the preceding days, Elaine had been undecided about how much and with whom she would share regarding her possible cancer. When she decided to speak openly about this with the others in her community, Elaine was moved by their sincere concern, shown in sensitive ways that she could not have imagined. Knowing that she can depend upon their understanding and support gives Elaine new strength. She thanks the Lord for the great gift of their love and decides to continue to share openly with them as the medical process develops. Experiencing the encouragement that she finds in the accompaniment of others, Elaine also decides to call her spiritual director and to meet more often in the coming weeks.

As she walks, Elaine also considers her prayer in the last few days. She has always spent time in prayer at the beginning of the day. These past two days, however, have been special. Her morning prayer has been a time of tears and of experiencing the Lord's loving presence in a new way. While others marvel that Elaine is able to continue her customary life and work as the operation draws nearer, she knows that her deepest strength derives from God, whose love she senses in her prayer. Elaine understands that prayer will be key in the days ahead. She decides that she will discuss with her spiritual director how to pray in these difficult circumstances. As her walk concludes, Elaine finds a quiet trust filling her heart, deeper than her very real fear. She knows that the God who loves her will be at her side — in her operation and beyond.

Elaine prays the examen in a time of interior turmoil, and through it she increasingly encounters God in the midst of personal crisis. Step five of the examen proves profoundly beneficial for her. By looking *back* over her experience of the past two days, Elaine is already able to take efficacious spiritual action regarding the days that lie *ahead*. We may expect that Elaine will continue to gain spiritual wisdom and peace as she prays her morning and evening examen in the days to come.

In each of these widely varied situations and in many others we might consider, the persons involved attain clarity for the future through a prayerful review of their spiritual experience during the preceding day or days. The power for spiritual growth in step five is evident.

The practice of step five: Renewal

Step five grows naturally out of the earlier steps in the examen and adds a new richness to them. Ignatius's directive is simple: allow the past (steps one through four) to illuminate the future (step five). Step five gives *insight* to a love that searches daily for spiritual growth; it is the Ignatian answer to the longing for such growth in hearts that seek God. This final step in the examen is the space for daily *creativity* in the Lord.

Like the former steps, step five also involves both human initiative ("to propose amendment") and God's freely given gift ("with God's grace"). Which spiritual initiatives will lead most surely to growth? What specifically shall we undertake as we prepare for the coming day? How may we hope to choose wisely among so many possibilities? Will we be able to live concretely the newness we seek? Our hope in step five, as throughout the entire examen, is founded on the richness of *God's grace*. With trust in that power we are confident, like Paul, that we "can do all things" (Phil. 4:13). Once again the *relational* quality of the examen is evident — the human person and God acting together in a partnership of love. In praying step five we ask for grace both to *see* clearly which initiatives God desires us to choose and to *practice* those initiatives effectively in the coming day.

Step five will often — though not always — be concerned with seemingly small initiatives, "small" enough that they may pass unnoticed by others: Joan's decision to look for brief moments of reflective awareness, Kevin's choice to review his many activities, Elaine's resolve to adapt her prayer to her changed circumstances. Yet most of life, and the greater part of the spiritual life as well, is lived precisely through such "small" events: the thousand choices and actions that constitute our days and our lives. Step five, in a way specifically its own, is the spiritual tool for progress in these multiple and spiritually decisive "small" events of the day.

Experience reveals the remarkable power for growth in the faithful practice of step five. Through it we discover where God is leading as our relationships develop and change in life. Through it we find God's call in new responsibilities. Through this step we grasp the meaning of new situations of health, in the family, or at work. Through the practice of step five we move forward amid the complexities of life with growing peace and surety; we discover that our God is for us today, as for the pilgrim people of old, a "pillar of cloud" and a "pillar of fire" (Exod. 13:22), a God walking faithfully at our side and leading in endlessly new ways to the fulfillment of the promise that is our hope.

Chapter Eight

Flexibility

The soul that wanders, Spirit led,
becomes, in His transforming shade,
the secret that she was in God,
before the world was made.

— Jessica Powers[1]

The examen and the individual

In the preceding chapters we have explored with some care each of the five steps of the examen. Understanding these steps is indispensable for the prayer of Ignatian examen, and no adequate treatment of the Ignatian examen can prescind from this. Most fundamentally, these steps articulate the space that our hearts enter whenever they pray a *Christian* examen. We know that we depend on grace for this as for all prayer, and so we ask for that grace. When we review the day, our hearts discover the concrete signs of God's love and give thanks for that love. We look to see how we have responded to the Lord's love, asking forgiveness where necessary. Then the light of today's examen assists us in pursuing with the Lord how we may grow in the day to come. Ignatius's five steps are not artificially construed but rather express what springs spontaneously from our hearts in the dialogue with God that is the examen.[2]

Now that we have described these steps, however, several questions of importance arise: How are these steps to be prayed in practice? Are they to be followed in sequence? Always to be followed in sequence? Should each step be prayed every time we make the examen? Should each be equally emphasized in our examen? Might one step be more important than another? Is the importance of each in relation to the others a constant? Might this too vary day by day? In the light of such questions, then, how should we view these five steps in the concrete praying of the examen? Obviously our answers will be fundamental to our practice of the Ignatian examen itself.

> How are these steps to be prayed in practice? Are they to be followed in sequence?...Might one step be more important than another?

Certainly, as we have seen, there is an inherent logic to the ordering of the five steps. To know in a tangible way that we are loved (step one) is for Ignatius the foundation of all prayer. Rooted anew in this relationship, we ask God for light and strength (step two), and we review our response to that love (step three), a review that flows into the healing encounter of forgiveness (step four) and which, with the insight gained, seeks new growth in the future (step five). We may choose to pray the steps in this order and may find them most fruitful when so prayed.

Especially when first learning the examen, we may do well to pray the steps in this way. We are blessed to share in a rich spiritual tradition of prayer born of the experience of great figures of holiness, and wisdom suggests that we allow this tradition to instruct us as we embark upon our own journey of prayer. Once these steps and their structure as a whole have been deeply experienced and assimilated, we may more surely, because of that grounding, pursue a creatively personal path in this prayer.

How long might this period of initial learning last? When may we judge that we have assimilated in *practice* the Ignatian meaning of the examen? When will our examen be truly enhanced by personal adaptations to this prayer? Such decisions will emerge with the practice itself of the examen, and, like much else in the life of prayer, will benefit from the counsel of experienced spiritual guides.

Ignatius's principle regarding prayer in general applies also to the prayer of examen: "in the point in which I find what I am seeking, there I will rest, without anxiety to move forward until my heart is satisfied" (*SpirEx*, 76). To this counsel we may add Ignatius's further teaching that "it is not much knowing that fills and satisfies the soul, but rather the feeling and tasting of things interiorly" (*SpirEx*, 2). The examen is most transforming when prayed with such attentiveness to the call of the Spirit within the five steps, and with the freedom to follow that call "without anxiety to move forward until my heart is satisfied."

This Ignatian principle essentially answers the questions raised above. The true "spiritual director" of our examen is the Spirit, and it is the Spirit's lead that we most fruitfully follow in praying the examen. David Townsend writes:

> Traditionally, as has been seen, there are five aspects or moments to the Examen, and on any one occasion perhaps one or more of these aspects will predominate. So these five aspects are not a syllabus to be got through. I give any one of these aspects the time I desire and need.[3]

Some brief examples will serve to illustrate this point.

In the freedom of the Spirit

A married man is praying his examen in the evening. This day, he and his wife have resolved a mutual tension in a manner that leaves both deeply happy. This wonderful gift and the desire to express gratitude to God for it fill his heart as he now prays the examen. This man will do well to "rest" in step one of the examen "without anxiety to move forward" through the subsequent steps until his heart "is satisfied"; his examen this day may well consist primarily in experiencing the love of the Giver through this gift and in a heartfelt response of gratitude to the Giver. The blessings and the spiritual newness that will flow from such an examen are clear.

A young woman is faced with an important decision regarding her future. Her decision will have significant consequences for her life. Throughout the day she experiences fluctuations of attraction, resistance, desire, and anxiety as she considers the different options. She seeks to choose according to the desire of the Lord she loves, but does not see clearly where the Lord is leading her. As she prays her examen this day, she may feel a special desire to "rest" in step two, seeking light and strength to understand the stirrings of her heart and how the Spirit is operative in them.

A priest experienced difficulty in relating with one of the parish staff during a meeting earlier in the day. This is not the first time he has felt this tension, and he senses it growing within him, diminishing his energy to serve the parish. The experience of the meeting reveals to him a special need to understand this tension and to seek in the Lord a clarity that will permit him to resolve the tension with wisdom and love. The priest may well feel called this day to focus his examen primarily on step three, praying specifically for deeper insight regarding this tension "without anxiety to move forward until [his] heart is satisfied."

A successful professional woman, a dedicated person who loves the Lord, attends Mass on Sunday in her parish. A visiting priest celebrates the Mass and tells in his homily of his work among the poor. The woman is deeply struck as she listens to his message. She realizes that she has seldom considered the needs of the poor in other countries and closer at hand in her own city. She begins to consider whether God desires that in some way she place her professional skills at the service of the disadvantaged. As this woman prays her examen this day, she may feel particularly called to step four: to ask God's forgiveness for that blindness and to ask for strength to love the poor in a concrete way.

A man is flying home the following day for a gathering of his parents, siblings, and relatives. He knows that some of these family relationships will be difficult and that he will need sensitivity and strength in the Lord to love as he desires. In his examen, this man may find the fifth step especially important, planning with the Lord how to love genuinely during his visit with his family.

In praying the examen, then, we may feel the Spirit drawing us to one or more of the steps with a particular insistence. If so, we will do well to heed that drawing and to pray the examen accordingly. If we feel no such specific call within the five steps, then we may simply pray the steps in sequence as Ignatius outlines them, ready to remain "in the point in which I find what I am seeking . . . without anxiety to move forward until my heart is satisfied."

Creative fidelity

Like all faithfully practiced prayer, the examen will develop, deepen, and simplify over time. This is not the simplicity of mere lack of understanding, but rather the fruit of sure learning and diligent application. When this development is authentic, such simplification will entail greater and not less fruitfulness in the prayer of the examen. Because these persons truly understand the examen and have assimilated it through persevering practice, they are likely to pray it with what we may call "creative fidelity." The content of the examen will remain, but may be expressed in personal ways. Some examples will clarify a few of the many forms this simplification may assume.

One such person says of the examen: "It does not have to be complicated. It is sort of being with the Lord and asking: How did we live the day together? Happy? Sad? What happened? What do you want me to see? How shall we plan for tomorrow?" The essence of the examen is present in the simplicity of this approach.

The relational quality of the examen is strongly present to this person: "It is sort of *being with* the Lord.... What do *you* want *me* to see?" The prayer is pervaded with *asking God* for the growth that is sought: "It is ... *asking: how* did we live.... *What* do you want.... *How* shall we plan ...?" The review of the day is central in this examen: "How did we *live the day* together? Happy? Sad? *What happened?* What do you want me to see?" This person looks at both the events of the day ("What happened?") and the movements experienced in the heart ("Happy? Sad?") as these events took place. The fourth step is certainly implicit in this person's formulation of the examen; such a profound relational sensitivity will include seeking the healing encounter of forgiveness when appropriate. Finally, having reviewed the day with the Lord, the person looks with initiative to the coming day: "How shall we plan for *tomorrow?*" This is the examen of one who has found a personal and creatively faithful approach to it.

Another person of long experience with the examen says yet more succinctly: "My examen at night is just to be with the Lord and say: 'Lord, help me to know my day as you know it. Help me to see what you see.' Then I look over the day." This yet more compact formulation again contains the essential aspects of the examen. There is a foundational consciousness of relationship with God: "My examen ... is just to be with the Lord.... " Petition for an insight that exceeds human capacity alone underlies the entire prayer: "Lord, help me to see.... Help me to know.... " This person then reviews the day in a generally chronological fashion as Ignatius suggests.

A response to the insight gained from this review is implicitly present in the words used. Once this person knows the past day *as the Lord knows it,* the heart will respond and clarity for growth in the coming day will result. The rich simplicity of this formulation contains, explicitly and implicitly, the core of the examen.[4]

A priest in his late seventies describes the prayer he makes as each day ends, which he continues in moments of wakefulness during the night:

I converse with God about the day I've spent, how it went, where I failed God or my neighbor, what graces came my way, and how well I used them. I like to talk to God about the people I encountered that day, in person, on the phone, through e-mail or snail mail....

Then I turn to the coming day, if God should grant it. I recall the intention for the Mass I will celebrate. It may be for a deceased brother Jesuit, or for a relative with cancer, or for our country in this time of national crisis. I talk to God about that intention. I bring God up to date on where I am politically, charitably, socially. I must admit I do much of the talking. But sometimes God does get through. I begin to see things more clearly. I realize there were times I was hasty in judgment or insensitive in action. I see new ideas opening up before me on how I can contribute to the graces God spreads through his Church, particularly through its sacramental life.[5]

Once more the steps of the examen are present. This man too has found his own way to pray the examen fruitfully.

Thus the examen is prayed according to its authentic nature (fidelity) and yet in keeping with the individual drawings of each person (creativity). The presupposition of this creativity is a solid grounding in the examen itself: sound assimilation of the steps — gratitude, petition, review, forgiveness, and renewal — in understanding and in practice. In this way, the sure richness of the tradition becomes life-giving for the individual in the present.

Both in our initial learning and in any personal adaptation of the examen, the accompaniment of another or of others who share this journey will be highly beneficial. We will discuss this point in the following part of this book.

PART THREE

CONDITIONS

Chapter Nine

The General Setting
of the Examen

O, learn to read what silent love hath writ.
To hear with eyes belongs to love's fine wit.
— Shakespeare

The importance of the setting

Thus far in our reflections we have focused on the prayer of the
examen itself: its five different steps and the flexible use of these
steps. In Ignatian terms, we have considered the nature of the
examen as a "spiritual exercise" of prayer.

A reading of the *Spiritual Exercises* reveals, however, that when
Ignatius presents his various spiritual exercises, he regularly accompanies them by what he calls *additions:* auxiliary counsels
that help "to make the exercises more fruitfully and to find more
readily what we desire in them" (*SpirEx*, 73). Ignatius provides
a number of such counsels, applies them to each stage of prayer
in the Spiritual Exercises, and desires that these be constantly
recalled throughout this experience of prayer.[1] Ignatius clearly
considers that the fruitfulness of a spiritual exercise depends not
only on our activity during the prayer itself but also on the setting
that prepares, accompanies, and follows upon it. This setting, he
indicates, assists us in making the exercise "more fruitfully" and
helps us "to find more readily what we desire" in our prayer.

It seems evident that Ignatius would apply this same principle to the first-named of his spiritual exercises, the examen

(*SpirEx*, 1).[2] This is to say that the fruitfulness of our examen hinges not only upon the time itself when we pray the examen — the focus of our considerations thus far — but also upon other factors that shape the spiritual setting in which we pray it. Experience verifies in fact that these additional factors do significantly influence our actual praying of the examen and its fruitfulness. Wise spiritual choices with respect to them will indeed lead us "to find more readily what we desire" in the practice of the examen. In this part of our reflections, then, we will explore what these additional aids might be and how they may serve to increase the fruitfulness of our examen.

> In his Spiritual Exercises Ignatius always presumes the assistance of a competent spiritual guide in the process of discernment.

This is not an easy task to attempt in writing. As with much else in the life of prayer, these conditions apply differently to different people. Not all of these conditions will be equally possible or equally helpful for every person who prays the examen. Not all are equally important. Most likely any attempt to undertake all of them at once would be more overwhelming than useful. Each, however, is worthy of our reflection and of the question: Can this means help me to grow in my examen? In this chapter we will discuss those conditions that regard the general spiritual setting of the examen. In the following chapter, we will consider further conditions that concern the actual praying of the examen in itself.

Spiritual accompaniment

The prayer of examen is most difficult (not impossible!) and hardest to sustain when we are spiritually alone. The examen becomes easier to pray and more readily hope-filled when we are spiritually accompanied in its practice.

If indeed the prayer of examen is a matter not only of moral growth but also of discerning the spiritual stirrings of our hearts,[3] then the value of such spiritual accompaniment is evident. In his Spiritual Exercises Ignatius always presumes the assistance of a competent spiritual guide in the process of discernment, a need that remains even as we grow in a personal ability to discern:

> He or she can, by listening well, help us to notice and say for ourselves what we might never clearly uncover for ourselves unless we were trying to tell some trusted and interested listener — a listener who has adequate learning and experience to be of help.[4]

What form might this spiritual accompaniment take?

- Spiritual direction, that is, regular meetings with a capable spiritual guide, is a solidly attested element of our spiritual tradition and can be of great assistance in praying the examen.

- For some people, occasional meetings with an experienced spiritual companion may be the most realistic form of such spiritual accompaniment.

- Participation in groups of spiritual formation with qualified leadership may be another avenue to obtain such spiritual support.

- Conversation with spiritual friends who share the same journey can also be highly encouraging in the practice of examen.[5]

Such forms of spiritual accompaniment are all the more important for persons living in a culture that itself provides less spiritual "accompaniment" than in the day of Ignatius.

Competent spiritual accompaniment provides the answer to many of the difficulties that dedicated persons may encounter in praying the examen (*SpirEx,* 326). At times — as is true of the spiritual life in general — notwithstanding our sincere willingness and diligent efforts, we may feel discouraged as we pray the examen. The examen may not seem fruitful in the way we had hoped, and we may even find it disheartening in some measure. We may consequently experience a certain diminishment of our energy to continue in its practice. As all that we have discussed earlier indicates, there may be many reasons for such difficulties. The surest way to navigate safely through them is conversation with a capable spiritual companion. Without such conversation, we may tend simply to relinquish the prayer of examen in these times of difficulty. Aided by such conversation, these very struggles become stepping-stones to new growth in the examen and through it to broader growth in our spiritual lives.[6]

> The examen is prayer but a prayer that
> itself presupposes another level of prayer
> in our lives.

Here an important observation arises regarding the mutual relationship of spiritual direction and the examen. If, as we have said, our practice of the *examen* profits greatly from spiritual direction, the converse is also true: our experience of *spiritual direction* also benefits greatly when we bring to it the fruits of our examen. The practice of daily examen provides the ideal "raw material" for a dialogue between director and directee. It ensures that this dialogue will center on the truly important issues in the directee's spiritual life at this time, and that it will pursue spiritual clarity and strengthening precisely where these are most necessary for this person now. The practice of regular examen infuses continual freshness into director and directee's sharing as together, over the years, they seek to follow the lead of the endlessly creative Spirit.[7]

Examen and our life of prayer

A glance at Ignatius's practice of examen on March 12, 1544, reveals that his prayerful review occurs within a day marked by various times of prayer. Ignatius prays upon rising, prays as he prepares for Mass, prays throughout the Mass itself, prays again after the Mass ... a prayer in which Ignatius meets the God "who loves me more than I love myself." From the richness of that communion with God in habitual times of prayer, the desire for ongoing communion with God throughout the day is born. It is this desire, as we have seen, that fuels the practice of examen. Our relationship with God in faithful daily prayer is the fertile soil in which a fruitful practice of the examen takes root and grows.

As Aschenbrenner so clearly notes, the examen is prayer but a prayer that itself presupposes another level of prayer in our lives.[8] Every step, then, that we take to grow in relationship with God through faithful prayer prepares the ground for our practice of examen. Is it superfluous to suggest once more that this might be profitably discussed with a spiritual guide? Or with others who share the same longing?

As with the examen and spiritual direction, here too a principle of mutual benefit holds.[9] Loving communion with God in formal times of prayer (meditation on Scripture, Mass, the Liturgy of the Hours, *lectio divina,* and other forms of prayer) awakens the desire to find that God of love throughout the day as well, and so leads to the examen. The examen in turn expands that relationship of love beyond the formal times of prayer and into the concrete activity of the day. In this way the formal times of prayer are not only occasional welcome moments of communion with God, but also flow more easily from and into the day of which they are a part, much as we see in Ignatius's March 12, 1544.

These are not just words. When our hearts rejoice to encounter God in habitual and faithfully observed times of prayer and, consequently, yearn to experience that communion more frequently and more deeply throughout the day as well, then we are ready for the practice of examen.

Developing the contemplative capacity

The depth of Ignatius's reflective capacity as exemplified on March 12, 1544, can easily evoke in the observer a certain sense of marvel. And the question we quoted earlier might well become our own: "Is it really possible to live this way?" Certainly, as we have seen, Ignatius himself did not begin this way; his March 12, 1544, represents the mature fruit of years of progressive development in the capacity to *notice* the spiritual stirrings of his heart.

As John Veltri aptly writes: "To reflect on one's own experiences to discover spiritual movements is a developed skill."[10] The developing of that skill is a normal part of growth in the prayer of examen. Classic theology teaches that the work of God's grace presupposes and further enriches all that is human. In terms of the examen, then, whatever increases our *human* capacity to notice experience around and within us simultaneously increases our capacity to notice, with the aid of God's grace, our *spiritual* experience as well.

- Noticing our surroundings as we walk

- listening attentively to the beauty of music in the room where we sit

- delighting in the smile and conversation of one we love

- peacefully contemplating the flames in a fireplace with a friend at our side

- silently gazing at a bird rising in flight

- observing cultural patterns as they emerge in the society around us

... noticing, seeing, contemplating, perceiving the reality that surrounds us and its resonance within us: all of this creates the human space for the prayer of examen.

Anne Morrow Lindbergh writes in her diary for May 30, 1932:

A quiet day, cool and sunny. C[harles] and I walked in garden, played with dogs. Elisabeth and I on the terrace talking. . . . I feel as though I wanted just to sit in the sun, outdoors, and let waves of green oak leaves and waves of small insect sounds, small rustlings and stirrings, pour into me, fill up all the wrinkles and cracks, make a smooth blank cool surface over everything. Then let impressions and thoughts come back clearly on that satin surface. But I do not want now to read or think or work; I just want to be filled up to the brim with quiet.[11]

Henri Nouwen reveals the same capacity to *notice* in the following passage that arises, remarkably, from the sight of a busy intersection in a large city:

Recently I was standing at the corner of Bloor and Yonge streets in downtown Toronto. I saw a young man crossing the street while the stoplight turned red. He just missed being hit by a car. Meanwhile, hundreds of people were moving in all directions. Most faces looked quite tense and serious, and no one greeted anyone. They were all absorbed in their own thoughts, trying to reach some unknown goal. Long rows of cars and trucks were crossing the intersection or making right and left turns in the midst of the large pedestrian crowd.

I wondered: "What is going on in the minds of all these people? What are they trying to do, what are they hoping for, what is pushing them?" As I stood at that busy intersection, I wished I were able to overhear the inner ruminations of all these people. But I soon realized that I didn't have to be so curious. My own restlessness was probably not very different from that of all those around me![12]

This is the language of one who has grown in the capacity to *notice* experience around and within himself: "I saw.... I wondered.... I soon realized...." And this is the interior human space into which the grace-inspired prayer of examen enters, further enriching this space with its own spiritual attentiveness.

Nouwen's awareness of *exterior* experience ("I saw...") guides him to awareness of his *interior human* experience ("My own restlessness...") and, finally, to *spiritual* awareness as his heart now lifts to God on the crowded street corner:

Why is it so difficult to be still and quiet and let God speak to me about the meaning of my life? Is it because I don't trust God?...Is it because I wonder if God really is there for me? Is it because I am afraid of God? Is it because, deep down, I do not believe that God cares what happens at the corner of Yonge and Bloor?

Still there is a voice — right there, in downtown Toronto. "Come to me, you who labor and are overburdened, and I will give you rest. Shoulder my yoke and learn from me, for I am gentle and humble in heart and you will find rest for your soul. Yes, my yoke is easy and my burden light" (Matt. 11:28–30).

Can I trust that voice and follow it? It is not a very loud voice, and often it is drowned out by the clamor of the inner city. Still, when I listen attentively, I will hear that voice again and again and come to recognize it as the voice speaking to the deepest places of my heart.[13]

How many such "street corners" are there in our day? How many relational interactions in our family, in our community, in our workplace, in our Church, in our world? How many events that, as Ignatius says, "hour by hour, or from one period of time to another" fill our day? In how many ways will we hear God

speaking to us through them if, like Nouwen, we "listen attentively"? How often, if we are humanly and spiritually watchful,
will we "hear that voice again and again and come to recognize
it as the voice speaking in the deepest places" of our hearts? This
is, exquisitely, the practice of examen.

As our capacity to notice interior and exterior *human* experience grows, we are correspondingly prepared to notice specifically
spiritual experience as well: in Ignatian terms, spiritual consolation and spiritual desolation, with their corresponding thoughts
(*SpirEx,* 316–17). In her examen after her weekday Mass, Susan
notices how "God's love is very real for her at this moment"
(spiritual consolation). She also remembers that on the preceding morning "God had seemed far away and she had felt little
energy for spiritual things" (spiritual desolation), such that she
had delayed an act of service to a coworker. As she prays her
examen Susan is now able to grasp the meaning of both spiritual experiences and understands how to respond appropriately
to both.[14]

Can all dedicated persons develop this ability to *notice* where
God is present in their daily experience? Aschenbrenner describes
the examen as a spiritual reality that is "gradually experienced
in faith" and as a prayer that takes place within "the Christian
consciousness, formed by God and His work in the heart as it confronts and grows within this world and all of reality." He writes
of "the necessary gradual adaptation" of the prayer of examen
to our "stage of development and the situation in the world"
in which we find ourselves.[15] We pray the examen as we do all
prayer, according to the God-given richness of the individual per-
sonality that is ours and according to how God is leading us in
prayer *now.* If we do so, our practice of examen will gradually
develop and with it, our capacity for spiritual awareness.[16]

Chapter Ten

The Specific Setting of the Examen

*God waits like a beggar who stands motionless
and silent before someone who will perhaps
give him a piece of bread. Time is that waiting.
Time is God's waiting as a beggar for our love.*
— Simone Weil

Beginning and concluding the examen

In our last chapter we discussed the conditions that create a favorable background for the examen in general. We turn now
to several "additional" conditions that may assist us when we
actually pray the examen. As in the preceding chapter, we are
speaking of conditions to be utilized and adapted as each person
finds personally advantageous. Each condition is worthy of our
consideration and may be beneficial in our search for growth in
the prayer of the examen. The first of these concerns *transitions:*
the spiritual ways that we choose to begin and to conclude this
time of prayer.

Entering the prayer of examen

The time we reserve for the examen may follow immediately upon
intensely absorbing activity or upon a gentler space of interior
quiet. In either case — more so in the first, yet still in both — a
fitting mode of transition into the formal time of examen contributes greatly to a fruitful praying of the examen itself. And
because, as we have so often noted, the examen is fundamentally

relational, the ideal transition consists in conscious awareness of God, who is present to us as we pray the examen.

Ignatius himself began his prayer with this living awareness of God's loving presence to him. An eyewitness tells of how Ignatius used to pray on the open terrace of the community's house in Rome:

> He would stand there and take off his hat; without stirring he would fix his eyes on the heavens for a short while. Then, sinking to his knees, he would make a lowly gesture of reverence to God. After that he would sit on a bench, for his body's weakness did not permit him to do otherwise. There he was, head uncovered, tears trickling drop by drop, in such sweetness and silence, that no sob, no sigh, no noise, no movement of the body was noticed.[1]

Ignatius begins his prayer with a brief moment in which he simply absorbs the joyful reality of God's presence to him. His awareness of God's loving gaze upon him fills him with "sweetness and silence," and moves him deeply and surely into the prayer to follow.

When in his *Spiritual Exercises* Ignatius counsels such a transition into prayer, he is evidently speaking from his own rich experience of prayer. Ignatius invites us, on the threshold of our formal time of prayer, to pause "for the time I would take to pray an Our Father" and "with my understanding raised on high" to consider "how God our Lord looks upon me" (*SpirEx,* 75). This transitional space need not, Ignatius tells us, be overly lengthy: "the time I would take to pray an Our Father." As Ignatius's words further indicate, what we consider during this brief time is how *God looks* upon us. As so often in Ignatian prayer, the focus is not primarily on our own activity but above all on what *God* is doing: here on what God is doing *now* as I begin my time of prayer. This transition is profoundly relational; before all else we become aware simply of *being with* the God who is looking upon us.[2]

How does "God our Lord look upon me" as I begin to pray my examen? If the unseen God is revealed to us in Jesus (John 1:18), then we may rephrase this question as follows: how does *Jesus* look upon those who approach him with humble and sincere hearts? Jesus looks upon Nathaniel and that look tells Nathaniel that he is deeply known and loved; it is a look that changes Nathaniel's life (John 1:48). Jesus sees Levi, and his look gives fresh meaning to Levi's existence (Mark 2:14). Jesus sees a woman in tears, and her tears are transformed into the joy of life restored (Luke 7:13). A man approaches Jesus, and the Gospel tells us that "Jesus, looking at him, loved him" (Mark 10:21). Jesus sees a woman burdened for eighteen years with an illness; she is set free and praises God (Luke 13:12–13). Jesus looks upon Peter in his time of utter failure, a look that leads to tears and to renewal in a love that will never again be shaken (Luke 22:61). All of this may be summarized in the words of John of the Cross: "the look of God is love and the pouring out of gifts."[3]

How does "God our Lord look upon me" now as I begin to pray my examen? Is there any better way to enter the examen than to pause briefly like Ignatius to consider this divine look, which is "love and the pouring out of gifts" upon me?[4] Experience will reveal to us the richness and the blessing that this transitional step adds to our examen.

As so often in his pedagogy of prayer, Ignatius simply indicates what experience, his own and others, has shown to be helpful without further specification of precisely how this indication is to be used in practice.

• One woman prays a short formal prayer, an Our Father, the Soul of Christ, or a prayer of Thomas Merton, and finds that in this way she enters the living presence of the Spirit.

• A man simply becomes aware of Father, Son, and Spirit, slowly pronouncing each divine name and so entering into communion with the living God.

◆ Another person recalls the scriptural words that "Jesus, looking at him, loved him" (Matt. 10:21) and feels that gaze of love personally as he lifts his heart in prayer.

How will each of us experience the loving look of God upon us as we come to the examen? How will we choose to pray this transitional moment? Creativity and reflection upon our experience will assist us in discovering our personal way of crossing this spiritual threshold into a fruitful prayer of examen.

Concluding the prayer of examen

In outlining the five steps of the examen, Ignatius also considers the transition out of the formal time of examen and into our more habitual activity. Again he does so succinctly, in this case simply mentioning the prayer of the Our Father (*SpirEx*, 43). Here as throughout the Spiritual Exercises, Ignatius suggests that heart-to-heart conversation ("colloquy") with God flow into and conclude with a classic formula of prayer (*SpirEx*, 54, 63, etc.). This brief classic prayer assists in the transition from the quiet communion of formal prayer to the more active space to follow. In this way the formal time of prayer does not end abruptly; rather it concludes gently, respecting our human need for transitional space when our hearts have encountered another person deeply. Applied to the examen, Ignatius's mention of a concluding Our Father suggests that our examen will be enriched if we explore spiritually helpful ways of transitioning out of our formal time of examen. The Our Father itself, a prayer that Cyprian tells us is "overflowing with spiritual strength" and is "a summary of heavenly teaching" in which "nothing is omitted that may be found in our prayers and petitions,"[5] may constitute a helpful transition for us. Certainly it is an exquisitely *relational* way to complete a prayer that is itself so profoundly relational.

We may, like Ignatius himself, choose other classic prayers that appeal to us as we conclude our examen.[6] We may adopt still other ways that assist us in making this transition fruitfully.

- A man offers a brief prayer of praise as he ends his examen.

- A woman concludes her examen by repeating several times a phrase that tells God of her love and fills her with a sense of that divine loving presence; she then prays a Glory Be.

- A priest expresses in his heart his thanks to God for the blessing of the examen just prayed.

The Ignatian pedagogical principle — experience accompanied by reflection on that experience — applies once again here. Ignatius's concise mention of a transition out of the prayer of examen suggests that this transition merits, at least briefly, our creative consideration.

"Where can I pray the examen?"

Already in this book we have noted a variety of places where the examen may be prayed fruitfully: in church after Mass, on a commuter train or a bus, during a walk for daily exercise, in a library before a time of study, in the quiet of a community chapel, in an office between meetings or on lunch hour, in the silence of one's room, in a car waiting for another to arrive . . . the possibilities are endless.

- One priest makes his examen seated in his armchair, a cup of coffee at hand.

- A spiritual director advises her directee, a mother with small children, to pray her examen in the bathroom with the door locked, the one space of quiet she can find in the day.

- A man whose office work involves little physical movement chooses to pray the examen while walking in a quiet place outdoors. Another man, whose day involves constant movement, opts rather to pray the examen in the calm of his room.

- A woman creates a prayer corner in her apartment with an icon and a candle, and there prays her examen.

- Another woman sits in the peace of a church for her examen, alive to the Lord's Eucharistic presence.

- A priest stops in the rectory chapel before supper, prays Evening Prayer, and then reviews his day with the Lord.

- A man whose day is packed with commitments converts long red lights and stopped traffic into times of examen.

- A husband and wife pray the examen together in their room as their day concludes.

Julien Green confides to his diary that "a blazing fire is a wonderful company. It helps one to think, it flickers, it blazes, it is there."[7] Joseph Tetlow describes his own reflective experience in these words:

A bungalow with a glassed-in porch on the bank of the silted Tangipahoa River. Spring flood, 1971. Joe Tetlow sits and stares into the roiling water through the grey Spanish-moss beards on emerald cypresses.... After a bout with walking pneumonia, he regularly comes to the bungalow on the Tangipahoa to stare into the middle distance and try to find his own center and his God.[8]

And Martin Buber depicts what he calls "The Busy Man's Prayer":

The Baal Shem said: "Imagine a man whose business hounds him through the streets and across the market-place the life-long day. He almost forgets that there is a Maker of the world. Only when the time for the Afternoon Prayers comes, does he remember, 'I must pray.' And then, from the bottom of his heart, he heaves a sigh of regret that he has spent his day on vain and idle matters, and he runs into a by-street and stands there, and prays: God holds him dear, very dear and his prayer pierces the firmament."[9]

Accompanied by the quieting presence of a softly burning fire, seated on a porch overlooking a river flanked with trees, standing on a by-street in a busy city: places to encounter God and pray the examen can be found almost anywhere. For each one of us there will be the right place or places.

I have advisedly asked the question "Where can I pray the examen?" in the first person singular. The answers to this question will be as varied as are the individual situations in which we live. The best place for the examen is the place that most assists in finding, as Ignatius so often repeats, "that which I wish and desire" in my prayer: the place in which I am most able to review in prayerful communion with God the day that I have lived. As throughout, the creativity that guides my choice is fueled by *desire,* a desire that will not permit me to choose a less suitable setting when one more effective for a fruitful examen is reasonably available.

What is that best place for me? Have I found it? Have I found it in my present circumstances?

"Do I have time for the examen?"

This is a fundamental question and one that I imagine has been present throughout to many readers whose lives involve pressing demands on their time. As wonderful as the prayer of examen may be, do *I* have time for it? Do I have time for it *regularly*? Is the examen reserved for those with less pressured lives or is there time for it in my life as well? These are real questions. For some they may be the most important questions if they are to undertake the prayer of examen.

Ignatius himself in describing the examen says nothing regarding length of time for this prayer (*SpirEx*, 43).[10] We find here once more that freedom of application to individual circumstances already so often evident in Ignatius's approach to the examen. Still, others before us have asked and answered these same questions. A brief glance at their answers, past and present, may assist us in charting our personal course in this regard.

A look at the tradition

Though the examen is for all persons in all walks of life, nonetheless a rapid review of the specifically Jesuit tradition with respect to these questions will provide a base from which to explore adaptations to the many vocations we share within the Church. In 1975 the Society of Jesus summarized its own tradition with regard to the examen in the following way:

> Twice daily the examination of conscience should be made, which, in accord with Ignatius' intent, contributes so much to discernment regarding our entire apostolic life, to purity of heart, and to familiarity with God in the midst of an active life. In accord with the approved tradition of the Society, it is recommended that it last a quarter of an hour.[11]

The Jesuit, thus, "in accord with the approved tradition of the Society" is to pray the examen twice a day, each time dedicating a quarter of an hour to this prayer. One reading of Ignatius's own text in the *Spiritual Exercises* (no. 43, third point) suggests that these two daily times of examen are, first, near the midpoint of the day and, second, in the evening hours.[12] Certainly, the practice as described here speaks eloquently of the importance the Jesuit tradition accords to the examen. Ample time is given to the examen because it is a prayer that "contributes so much to discernment regarding our entire apostolic life," which builds "purity of heart," and which fosters "familiarity with God in the midst of an active life." That these rich spiritual fruits are desirable for all disciples of the Lord is evident.

The tradition linked to the Ignatian Spiritual Exercises — and so to persons of all callings who make this retreat — manifests yet again the value of the examen, seen as a key means for sustaining the grace of the retreat in daily living. Diego Miró, writing not long after the death of Ignatius, suggests that the layperson who has experienced the Spiritual Exercises will profitably "make an examination of conscience for a quarter hour every day."[13] And

the Official Directory of 1599, in offering "Reminders for Someone Finishing the Exercises," includes "the daily examination of
conscience for a quarter hour."[14] In our own time, one author
reflects many in writing of the examen:

> Saint Ignatius of Loyola recommends that we make it a daily
> prayer by reserving about ten to fifteen minutes at the close
> of each day, or at some other moment when we can steal a
> bit of quiet from our busy schedules.[15]

Others simply counsel the daily prayer of the examen without
attempting to indicate any specific amount of time or moment in
the day for its practice.[16]

A look at our own reality

There is wisdom in all of these approaches. The variety among
them reflects the variety of callings in the Church and of individual circumstances within each of those callings. This tradition
manifests, however, the need for concrete personal choices with
regard to reserving time for the examen. Without such choices
the examen is unlikely to perdure as a practice in our lives; these
choices are the gateway to the richness of grace the examen offers
in our lives.

The key is *desire*. Persons who have encountered the God "who
loves me more than I love myself" and who daily reveals that
love through an outpouring of gifts, who have experienced "the
supreme good of knowing Christ Jesus" (Phil. 3:8) and long to
live in daily communion with the Lord they love, whose pas-
sion in life is to live the commandment of love (Mark 12:28–31)
with "a great spirit and generosity" (*SpirEx,* 5), will, like their
brothers and sisters of earlier and present generations, find time
to include the examen in their day. For such persons the answer
to our original question, "Do I have time for the examen?" is,
simply, a love-inspired "Yes."

What practical form will that "yes" of the heart assume in
our daily living? As always, the answers will be chosen according

to individual circumstances. And, as always, conversation with a spiritual guide can be of great value in making such choices effectively. With both of these observations in mind and subject to them, we may offer a few general observations regarding time and the examen.

> The variety among these approaches
> reflects the variety of callings in the
> Church and of individual circumstances.

If we are unsure of how to proceed, most often we will do well to begin with a shorter rather than a longer time. One man tells of learning about the examen during an Ignatian retreat. After the retreat he dedicated a half hour to it each evening, finding it a blessed and fruitful exercise of prayer. His practice of the examen endured for six months and then, perhaps predictably, faded. How much time can we give to the daily examen and reasonably hope to sustain this practice? It is best to begin with what seems solidly possible. As our practice of the examen grows, more daily time may be added should this appear helpful.

All the same, if we consider the prayerful richness of the five steps of the examen as we have already explored them — gratitude, petition, review, forgiveness, and renewal — the Ignatian examen evidently necessitates more than a quick minute or two of rapid reflection. The spiritual tradition described above further confirms this truth. There *is* a way of finding God through brief moments of discerning awareness during the day, and we will return to this grace-filled practice later in our reflections. Such brief moments, however, are different from and generally dependent upon a specifically chosen, unhurried time for the daily prayer of examen as we are discussing it here. Between the two positions, then — unsustainably lengthy or overly limited times for the examen — lies a healthy and practical spiritual balance, a balance that each of us is called to discover personally.

One further specific question regarding time is worthy of note: Is the last moment of the day the best time for the examen? For some of us it may be. For some in fact this may be the only real opportunity to pray the examen. Others may find the examen more effective when prayed earlier in the evening or in the day, and so when tiredness is less of a distraction.[17] As always, experience and reflection upon our experience will bring clarity. The options in this regard are many. George Washington Carver, a man of deep Christian faith whose selfless dedication to science blessed countless lives, writes:

> Back of my workshop there is a little grove of trees. One has been cut down. It makes a good seat. I have made it a rule to go out and sit on it at 4 o'clock every morning and ask the good Lord what I am to do that day. Then I go ahead and do it.[18]

- A married couple dedicates approximately seven or eight minutes to their examen each evening as their day is concluding.

- A woman religious chooses a quarter of an hour for her examen at a different time each day according to her varied apostolic commitments

... and the examples could be multiplied endlessly. As those already cited indicate, the possibilities in choosing times for the examen are broad. Dedicated persons in their varied callings will find their own way.

Journaling and the examen

In a church where I used to celebrate Mass from time to time, a woman volunteer would open the door when I rang the bell. She was in her late sixties and limited in her ability to walk; she was a woman of deep faith. She always seemed to have a smile, and one day I was bold enough to ask her how she managed to smile so invariably and so sincerely. My question itself evoked a smile.

She said that a few years earlier she had begun a practice that had made a great difference in her life. It was very simple. A friend had described her own habit of writing each evening five things for which she was grateful in the day.[19] This woman had liked the idea and had decided to try it. At first, she said, it was hard to find five things to write. Then as the months went by it became easier. "And now," she said, with that characteristic smile, "the list is endless. Every day."

Anne Morrow Lindbergh explains in the following way why she chose to write the thoughts that became her book *Gift from the Sea:*

> I began these pages for myself, in order to think out my own particular pattern of living, my own individual balance of life, work and human relationships. And since I think best with a pencil in hand, I started naturally to write.[20]

The same principle underlies both experiences cited here and many others we might add: that for some, perhaps for many of us, the exercise of *writing* our interior experience helps us to understand that experience itself more deeply. Such writing may also assist us in discovering patterns in our experience that we may not perceive in the day, but that emerge with clarity over time. One woman who keeps a journal of her daily examen says: "The writing allows me to go back and, by rereading, to reflect on my spiritual experience. I find this especially useful when I am in the process of making important decisions or when I notice certain tendencies developing in my life. But I write above all because I find that I can clarify my thoughts by writing."

Ignatius's written record for March 12, 1544, bears clear witness to his own practice of such journaling. The *Spiritual Diary* — which includes that March 12 — describes, in two notebooks, Ignatius's spiritual experience of a little over a year.[21]

Luis Gonçalves da Câmara, to whom Ignatius dictated his *Auto-biography,* writes of seeing Ignatius with an extensive packet of such personal notes in hand; of these he read to da Câmara only a part, unwilling to give da Câmara the written pages themselves.[22] Such testimony indicates that Ignatius himself found journaling of value in discerning the meaning of his spiritual experience.

The entries for some days in the *Spiritual Diary* are extensive; for others Ignatius writes only a few lines or even a single line. At times Ignatius uses abbreviations as he journals. And not only did Ignatius write his experience for each day; his reworking of the *Spiritual Diary* manuscript manifests his practice of returning attentively to what he had written when discerning an important matter, as during those days in 1544. The words Ignatius cancels or changes, the lines with which he encircles certain paragraphs he especially wishes to remember, and his copying of selections of his journal onto separate sheets, all witness to his attentive rereading of his spiritual journal. Both his writing and his rereading of his journal testify to the value Ignatius found in journaling as part of his striving for ongoing discerning awareness of God's action in his life.[23]

Spiritual practices, with all their richness,
benefit greatly from periodic renewal.

In the context of his Spiritual Exercises Ignatius notes that "the exercitant can be told to write down his ideas and movements."[24] Such in fact is common practice in giving and making the Ignatian retreat. José Calveras describes the review of prayer so central to the Spiritual Exercises (*SpirEx,* 77) and affirms: "The lights, inspirations, proposals and inclinations may be noted briefly in writing, after they have been well examined."[25]

Will all who pray the examen find such spiritual journaling helpful? Once again no single answer can be given. Here too the answer will vary according to the individuals who pray the examen. Certainly, given the experience of so many and given the witness of the tradition, the question is worth our consideration.

Would my prayer of examen be enriched if I were to note "briefly in writing" "the lights, inspirations, proposals and inclinations" that emerge from my review of the day with the Lord? Would occasional rereading of this journal assist me in perceiving more clearly where the Lord is leading at this time in my life? To see more specifically the obstacles that may diminish my spiritual energy to follow that call? To identify the measures that will best assist me in answering that call? Might such writing and rereading provide a clearer focus for both director and directee in a meeting of spiritual direction?

Our individual answers to such questions may be pursued though the Ignatian spiritual channels already familiar: experience, reflection on that experience, and conversation with the one or ones who accompany us spiritually on this journey.

Periodic renewal in the examen

A final consideration arises from the experience of dedicated people who pray the examen faithfully and have done so for years. Some with whom I spoke expressed both their appreciation of this prayer and their desire for fresh energy in their practice of it. One grace-inspired cause of this desire may simply be growth in the prayer of examen, and the fact that they are now ready to pray it in new and deeper ways.

A general principle regarding the entire life of prayer, however, may also be operative here: spiritual practices, with all their richness, benefit greatly from periodic renewal. Special times of retreat, spiritual reading or tapes, participation in a group of prayer, conversation with friends, or sharing with a spiritual director: there are many means for such periodic renewal, and they effectively foster ongoing growth in prayer. If from time to time we choose some such spiritual means specifically focused on re-newal in our prayer of examen, then our examen is likely to retain its vitality and to grow. Miguel Angel Fiorito suggests in fact that at least once in our lifetime we make a retreat centered entirely on the prayer of examen, explored in all its Ignatian richness.[26] This is only one of a wide variety of possible means toward periodic renewal in our prayer of the examen.

In such times of renewal, we may rediscover or learn more about various dimensions of the examen. Through examining our own examen, new perspectives will open and fresh energies be re-leased for growth in our practice of it. One instructive aspect of the interviews involved in writing this book was that *all* those I interviewed indicated after our conversation that simply *speaking about* their prayer of examen had given them new insight into it and renewed desire for it. Are there means of periodic re-newal that might also strengthen our prayer of examen? Creative consideration of such possibilities may significantly enhance our practice of this prayer.

PART FOUR

COURAGE

Chapter Eleven

Examen and the Courage to Love

*We never know how high we are
Till we are called to rise;
And then, if we are true to plan,
Our statures touch the skies.*
— Emily Dickinson

"I am sent to count your footprints"

Among "The Sayings of the Desert Fathers," in which history and legend mingle in teaching profound spiritual truths, we read of a man who went out into the desert to dedicate his life to God. He lived there for years, devoting himself faithfully to God's service through prayer and a life of great material simplicity. His dwelling was several miles from the nearest water, and daily he walked those miles to and from the source, carrying back the water he needed to live. Year followed upon year and he grew elderly in God's service.

But as those years passed, his heart gradually wearied of his service: the physical privations, the labor, the endless routine of one day utterly like the next. The long daily trek for water became the symbol of his weariness, and it was in walking those miles each day that he first began to consider surrendering the service of God he had pursued for so many years. Finally one day as he plodded across the desert under the burning sun, his heart weakened. The account tells us:

Once when he was going to draw water, he flagged and said to himself, "What need is there for me to endure this toil?

139

I shall come and live near the water." And saying this, he turned about and saw one following him and counting his footprints: and he questioned him, saying, "Who are you?" And he said: "I am an angel of the Lord, and I am sent to count your footprints and give you your reward." And when he heard him, the old man's heart was stout, and himself more ready, and he set his cell still farther from the water.[1]

Will such moments occur for us as well if we undertake the practice of examen? Will we find this prayer habitually welcome and blessed? Or might there be difficulties in the beginnings themselves or later along the way? If such difficulties occur, will they persist? Might we experience resistance to the examen at some point? Will we, like this man, after months or years of praying the examen find ourselves struggling to persevere with it?

If so, it is comforting to know that there is "an angel of the Lord" sent to count the footprints of our fidelity: to know that our efforts to pray the examen are precious and rewarded in God's sight. Nonetheless, this book would be incomplete were we not to discuss the struggles we may encounter in the practice of the examen, those times when this prayer will call for the *courage to love*.[2] "Love," Paul tells us, "is patient.... it bears all things . . . endures all things" (1 Cor. 13:4–7). The same Paul tells us that patience and faithfulness are among the fruits of the Spirit (Gal. 5:22). We may expect that the longing for God that moves us to pray the examen will sometimes call for these qualities of love and for these fruits of the Spirit.

The examen, as we have noted so often, is all about *relationship:* our relationship with God, whose love we experience with gratitude and to whose love our hearts desire to respond each day. Any authentic, deep, and enduring relationship of love calls at times for courage. A mother rises repeatedly in the night to assist her sick child; a son visits a failing parent daily after work, caring for his parent's needs; a priest interrupts his first moment of rest to answer an urgent call from the hospital; a teacher gives extra time at the end of a tired day to a student in special need; a husband cares for a wife who can no longer walk . . . the instances of such faithful love are many. Genuine love, the happiest reality in our lives, calls at times for courage.

Jean Vanier, speaking of trials in relationships, writes: "The times of trial which destroy a superficial security often free new energies which had until then been hidden."[3] In the prayer of the examen as in all prayer — which is simply a relationship of love — there will very likely be times when we will be called to love with faithful courage, a courage that will "free new energies which had until then been hidden."

Our awareness that the examen is God's gift rather than our accomplishment gives us the confidence expressed by Paul: "I have the strength for everything through him who empowers me" (Phil. 4:13). And experience teaches, as Thérèse of Lisieux says, that "God never refuses that first grace that gives one the courage to act; afterwards, the heart is strengthened and one advances from victory to victory."[4]

In this part of our reflections, then, we will consider the times when the prayer of examen may call us to a love that is patient and faithful. Having reviewed them, we will be the better equipped to progress through such times unfalteringly and indeed with spiritual benefit. Our discussion here will presume all that we have said thus far about the examen: solid understanding of the five steps, of their flexible use, and of the various conditions that assist in praying the examen fruitfully.

Beginnings

For many of us the discovery of the examen is a spiritually uplifting experience. Whether through a spiritual director, a retreat, a prayer group, a talk in the parish, a conversation with a friend, or even through a book like this, we learn of a way of praying that leads effectively toward that deeper, daily union with God that our hearts desire (Ps. 63:1); we also realize that this means of spiritual growth is within our grasp.

This is the time of the "first love" (Rev. 2:4) as this applies to the examen: the freshness and delight we experience in discovering a new means of spiritual progress. This same uplift of heart may also accompany a rediscovery of the examen, now understood in a way that enkindles new desire.[5] For some of us, perhaps for many, the attraction of this "first love" itself will move us to undertake and to persevere in the prayer of the examen.

But what if praying the examen hurts?

Even so, a certain creative effort may be necessary to decide about times and places for the examen and about the various conditions that facilitate its practice. Persevering initiative may be required to find some form of spiritual accompaniment — a group, a knowledgeable friend, an occasional or regular spiritual director — on this new journey of prayer. This early stage may also call for the willingness to persist in beginnings that feel uncertain, confident that, as Thérèse says, "God never refuses that first grace that gives one the courage to act."

Some people may find, as they begin to pray it, that the examen seems less effective than the writing and experience of others would appear to promise. They may doubt, then, whether the examen is indeed an efficacious prayer or, at least, whether it can be so for them. Should they experience such struggles, conversation with a competent spiritual guide would be highly beneficial. A variety of causes may underlie these initial hurdles, and such conversation assists greatly in surmounting them.

A basic principle of the entire spiritual journey, however, is very likely at work in such experiences. As John of the Cross writes so simply: "On this journey, we must always continue to walk if we are to arrive."[6] All human growth is subject to the law of time, and the prayer of examen is not exempted from this process. Something similar occurs the first time we touch the keys of a piano or speak our first words in a new language, or, even more to the point, converse for the first time with a new friend: these are only the beginnings of a fruitfulness that will surely grow if we persevere in the process. In fact, "On this journey, we must always continue to walk if we are to arrive."

The first experiences — difficult, rewarding, or a mixture of both — are the already blessed promise of further growth to come if we pray the examen with patient and faithful love. The *initial courage to love* in praying the examen is fertile soil for future growth in daily communion with the One who loves us here, today, infinitely, always.

The wounds of the heart

But what if praying the examen hurts? What if dedicated persons, convinced of the value of the examen and genuinely willing to pray it, find almost invariably that their examen impresses them with a sense of their own failure more than of God's warmly present love? Does this mean that the examen is not for them? How shall we understand such situations?

A woman tells of an expression that she once heard and loves, and which she often brings to her examen: "If you experience difficult moments when you feel totally separated from God, take off your shoes. You are standing on holy ground." Here, perhaps more than anywhere else in our reflections, we are truly standing on holy ground (Exod. 3:5). We will approach these struggles with great reverence for the mystery, the wonder, the richness, and the pain of human experience.

A man loves the Lord and seeks to place God at the heart of his life. Daily he dedicates time to prayer. He finds a spiritual director and meets regularly with him. He is conscious of serving the Lord in his work. He is intelligent, talented, and likeable. Others appreciate his presence, sense his genuine faith, and admire his valuable work.

He learns of the examen, knows that great figures of holiness attest to its worth, and decides to pray it daily. He does not take this commitment lightly and strives to be faithful to the practice of examen.

But this man has a secret. He suffers from an addiction, and the addiction leads to behavior that his conscience cannot condone. No one sees this, no one knows of this. Because of his deep sense of shame, he is unable to speak openly about this, not even with his spiritual director. At times he tries to speak more plainly but his shame inhibits him, and the director is unaware of the deep burden this man carries silently in his heart. Externally and in the eyes of all who know him, this man appears to be cheerful, purposeful, close to God, and successful in his work. Internally and in his own eyes, he lives in a deep pool of shame and guilt.

And every time he prays his examen, the same experience repeats. His *mind* accepts the value of the examen. He has learned the meaning of the steps and how to pray them. But every time the *feeling* of shame overwhelms him, and his experience of the examen is always the same. He inevitably focuses on something he has done wrongly in the day and cannot move beyond this. He says: "I beat myself up as I looked at the day. I was unable to look at the day and let it go." For him the examen does not seem to help. It is not a positive experience. It is rather a time when his underlying sense of shame and guilt before God surfaces and his heart feels pain.

Years pass in this way. At times he drops the practice of the examen altogether. At other times he tries again. Occasionally there are moments when he does sense God's closeness in prayer. Without such moments this man could not go on. But they are infrequent. They pass, and the power of the addiction returns. With that return, his sense of shame and his struggle with the examen also return.

Then a day of grace comes when the pain is too great. He knows that he can no longer live this way. He reaches out for help with his addiction and the behavior associated with it. He breaks the silence, and he reveals his hidden shame to a competent person. He joins a group of others who share the same struggle and meets regularly with them. For the first time he is able to speak openly with his spiritual director of this longstanding burden. The grip of the addiction slowly begins to lift.

Gradually there is a spiritual change as well. He begins to know himself, he says, "as a *loved* sinner," welcomed, redeemed, and embraced by God in his very struggle to grow.[7] His pain begins to become healing for others as well through his compassion, his words, and the understanding he shows them. Slowly too his prayer of examen begins to change. Some days, the old, shame-based pattern surfaces again. On his better days, he can truly pray the first step of the examen; he is now able to feel genuine gratitude in the presence of the Lord. "On these days," he says, "I can see the Lord's salvation at work in my life and in my recovery. I know that the Lord does love me in all this stuff."

Recently he found himself caught in a cycle of resentment as he made the examen: evening after evening the same heaviness, the same resentments, feeling helpless to find a way out. Then he met with his spiritual director and shared what he was experiencing in his examen. The director listened well, suggested several possibilities the man himself had not considered, and invited his directee to "keep looking and learning." "Our conversation," this man says, "gave me new hope with my examen."

I am deeply grateful to this man for sharing an experience of the examen in which he is surely not alone. How many others, when they stand in silence before the Lord, carry a secret in their hearts? How many others feel something of this shame, feel somehow less than they would wish to be when they approach God and so when they pray their examen as well? When we carry such secrets in our hearts, though we may understand and value the examen in itself, we may find, like this man, that when we actually attempt to pray it a feeling of shame dominates all else; then it is difficult to feel gratitude and painful to review the day. The examen becomes the *occasion* to feel something less perceived in the busyness of the day but always present in our hearts.

Persons who have this or a similar experience of the examen need to know, as this man's story shows, that *there is hope*. They need to know that freedom from an endlessly repeating pattern of painful examen is possible, and that human and spiritual re-sources for healing are available to them. They need to know that "amazing grace" can work in their lives as in the life of this man, leading them to the time when they can break the spiritual silence and their healing can begin.

But what if they feel unable, at this moment, to attempt such openness? What if the effort to speak seems as yet beyond their strength? Even now they can *pray* for that grace, asking it of the God who promises that "*Everyone* who asks, receives" (Matt. 7:8).[8] Simply to know that a path to freedom exists and that others have walked it before them may be itself the beginning of new hope, preparing the way to sharing and spiritual liberation. Then the struggle itself of their examen is indeed "holy ground"; it is the place where the Lord who is "gentle and lowly in heart" (Matt. 11:29) calls and unceasingly invites: "Come to me, all you who labor and are burdened, and I will give you rest" (Matt. 11:28).[9]

What will happen in this man's life if he perseveres on this path toward human and spiritual growth, faithfully using the means that he has now embraced? That growth will increase and, together with it, the fruitfulness of his prayer of examen. The "better days" will become more frequent and his new hope in his examen more deeply rooted.[10]

This story is a dramatic instance of painful struggle with the examen, a struggle rooted in profound shame; years passed before the self-opening that began a process of healing. However, on less dramatic levels as well something similar can occur in praying the examen.

In less consuming but still very real ways, other persons too may experience spiritual self-questionings. These questions are likely to surface during the examen, and these persons too will feel some uneasiness when they pray it. They may then believe that only two alternatives lie before them, both silently unhappy: to cease to pray the examen, or to continue to pray it with frequent discomfort of heart.

The way beyond this impasse lies in speaking with a competent spiritual guide (*SpirEx*, 326); for these persons this will be possible with a certain but not an excessive effort. Such sharing will often be the first step toward freedom and renewed energy in praying the examen. If through that sharing or through some other channel parallel to it they also learn the wisdom of Ignatius's rules for discernment,[11] these persons will find themselves increasingly equipped to respond effectively to such spiritual uneasiness.

In this way their very struggles with the examen become the occasion for new growth. At this point, their examen has truly become "holy ground."

Chapter Twelve

Examen and
Surrendering to Love

Keep Thou my feet; I do not ask to see
The distant scene — one step enough for me.
— John Henry Newman

Spiritual consolation and spiritual desolation

Throughout our reflections we have used Ignatius's language of *spiritual consolation* and *spiritual desolation* to describe respectively the uplifting or heavy affective movements our hearts may experience in the spiritual life (*SpirEx*, 316–17).[1] Both are part of every spiritual journey and both may enter our prayer of examen.

We have watched Ignatius pray his examen in times of profound spiritual consolation, even unto tears. When he reviews his early morning prayer on that March 12, 1544, Ignatius writes: "I felt much devotion, and from the midpoint on, there was much of it, clear, lucid, and, as it were, warm."[2] In describing his Mass that day he continues: "During one part of the Mass I felt much devotion and at times movements toward tears" (380). And after his struggle later that morning, spiritual consolation returns: "With this the darkness gradually began to lift and tears began to come" (382). Often Ignatius's prayer of examen is a remembrance and an experience of spiritual consolation, of joy in the Lord.

- One man describes his examen as "being in the presence of this Godhead, the Trinity" and as "experiencing this unconditional love." "It is," he says, "simply feeling loved," and continues: "The nice thing about it is that you discover that life is glorious."

- ◆ A woman speaks of her examen as "becoming more aware of God's presence" and as a "building up of a bank of gratitude" on which she can draw in more difficult times.

- ◆ Another tells of years during which her prayer of examen was "an intense and intimate love relationship with God."

Many who pray the examen describe the gratitude for God's love they feel as they pray it, and how that gratitude blesses the ending of their day. These are beautiful experiences of *spiritual consolation* in the prayer of examen; we receive them as gifts of God's love, and they strengthen us in that relationship of love.

What then of the times of *spiritual desolation* when our hearts feel heavier and God seems farther away?[3] How shall we pray the examen in these more difficult times?

Ignatius's experience on March 12, 1544, provides us with clear examples also of an examen prayed in such spiritual desolation. After the morning Mass on that day he writes: "I found myself utterly deserted and without any help, unable to feel the presence of...the Divine Persons" (380–81). Ignatius experiences himself as "so remote and so separated from them as if I had never felt their presence and never would again" (381). In fact, he says, "thoughts came to me at times against Jesus, at times against another [divine] Person" (381). He finds himself "confused with various thoughts" and writes: "I could find rest in nothing" (381).

Clearly these were difficult spiritual circumstances in which to pray the examen! It may be heartening to know that, like us, Ignatius too underwent such spiritually dark moments: the times when our hearts feel far from the Lord we love, when we feel "separated" from God, "without any help," and when our minds are spiritually "confused with various thoughts." Ignatius learns from his experience as we from ours, that every disciple of the

Lord will encounter spiritual desolation at various points on the spiritual journey.

Ignatius knows from long experience and grace-guided reflection that God permits such trials for a purpose of love: if we resist spiritual desolation with courage, that desolation is transformed into a source of spiritual growth (*SpirEx*, 322). A certain kind of spiritual maturity can only develop, normally speaking, through spiritual desolation experienced and resisted. On this March 12, in fact, only when Ignatius stops and examines his spiritual desolation does he realize that his desire in that moment is not in accord with God's desire. Blessed by this new clarity, Ignatius strives to conform his heart to God's desire; his spiritual desolation lifts, and he is confirmed in his discernment.

A woman experiences some measure of self-doubt and has been struggling recently to feel God's love for her personally. Some weeks earlier, after speaking with her spiritual director, she had renewed her practice of the daily examen. For her, the *practice of the examen itself* is the instrument of liberation from spiritual desolation. She writes:

> I feel now as if I was wandering through a jungle before I began the examen, and was wide open to every negative thought which could pretty freely take hold of me, since I wasn't paying attention. It was only when those thoughts got dark enough and consuming enough that I noticed that something was very wrong. But even then, I felt helpless to stop what was happening since I wasn't at all clear what it was....
>
> My "after" experience, that is, of making the examen daily, has let me see the problem much more clearly for what it is. The simple question of asking if certain thoughts or patterns of acting are leading me toward God or away from him is like shining a light into a dark room — one sees all sorts of things for what they are. The other thing it has let me see is "early warning signals" — the blindness that got me into

trouble in the first place.... I am very, very grateful that the Lord has been so patient, that he has given me such clear helps along the way, and that he has shown me so clearly what I need to do.

For this woman as for many of us, the prayer of examen — with the accompaniment at least occasionally of a spiritual guide — becomes an experience of spiritual freedom: "The simple question of asking if certain thoughts or patterns of acting are leading me toward God or away from him is *like shining a light into a dark room* — one sees all sorts of things for what they are." As her spiritual understanding grows, her darkness dissipates and gratitude wells up in her heart.

> If we resist spiritual desolation with
> courage, that desolation is transformed
> into a source of spiritual growth.

This woman's experience manifests the power of the examen in overcoming spiritual desolation (*SpirEx*, 319). She is a person who has grown in the ability to pray the third step of the examen (review) and is indeed more likely now to perceive "early warning signals" and so to resist spiritual desolation in its very beginnings (*SpirEx*, 325).[4] She is a person progressing in that patience and faithfulness which are the fruits of the Spirit's action in our hearts (Gal. 5:22), a person who is developing the courage to love through the practice of the examen.

At times, perhaps for extended periods of times, the examen will be a prayer of *spiritual consolation*. We will desire it and find its practice blessed. Through our daily examen we will feel and rejoice in God's love. We may expect, however, that in times of *spiritual desolation* the examen will feel less inviting. To know this in advance (*SpirEx*, 323), as we undertake the practice of the examen, prepares us to persevere faithfully through these difficult times and so to grow spiritually through them as God intends. With Ignatius (*SpirEx,* 320), we may be sure that God's grace will *always* suffice to stand firm in the trial (1 Cor. 10:13). Through such faithful perseverance, as Thérèse writes, "the heart is strengthened and one advances from victory to victory."

Letting go

On that March 12, 1544, Ignatius realizes at a certain point that his own desire contrasts with God's desires for him. And he writes:

> Once I recognized that I felt this inclination and that this was different from what God desired, I began to note this and to strive to move my heart toward what was pleasing to God. (382)

The love for the Lord that fills Ignatius's heart leads him, he says, "to strive to move my heart toward what was pleasing to God." When Ignatius perceives God's desire, he begins — not without effort — "to strive to move" his own heart toward communion with the heart of God. And, as he tells us, "With this the darkness gradually began to lift and tears began to come" (382). His earlier spiritual desolation lifts and consolation returns, providing clarity for his process of decision.

To pray the examen daily is to listen constantly for the "still small voice" (1 Kings 19:12) of God speaking in our hearts. The examen expresses our daily readiness *to hear God's desires* for our lives. Said in the words of Paul, to pray the examen is to confess that "Jesus is Lord" (Rom. 10:9) *every day* of our lives, eager to know his desires and to follow where he would lead us in the hours of our day. It is, like Ignatius, "to strive to move" our hearts toward the heart of the God whose love embraces us daily. To pray the examen is to surrender our lives increasingly to the Lord and to let ourselves be led because, like Ignatius, "we

have come to know and to believe in the love God has for us"
(1 John 4:16).

The prayer of the examen progressively leads to that transformation so tellingly depicted by John Henry Newman at a moment
when he was himself facing a new surrender to God's mysterious
leading in his life:

> I was not ever thus, nor prayed that Thou
> Shouldst lead me on.
> I loved to choose and see my path; but now
> Lead Thou me on![5]

"*I loved to choose* and see my path": this is the human ten-
dency toward self-sufficiency, toward seeking personal control in
the unfolding of our lives. A powerful transition, however, is occurring in the Newman who writes these lines: "but now / *Lead
Thou* me on!" The prayer of examen arises in hearts that desire
to say with Newman, "but now / Lead Thou me on," and that
desire this divine leading not only in the great decisions of their
lives but also in the concrete, daily, and "small" activities that fill
their days.

In a meditation completed thirteen days before his death from
pancreatic cancer, Joseph Cardinal Bernardin movingly describes
what he calls "letting go."[6] He writes:

One theme that arises on the surface more than any other
takes on new meaning for me now — the theme of letting go.

By letting go, I mean the ability to release from our grasp
those things that inhibit us from developing an intimate
relationship with the Lord Jesus.

Letting go is never easy. Indeed, it is a lifelong process.
But letting go is possible if we understand the importance of
opening our hearts and, above all else, developing a healthy
prayer life. (3)[7]

This is the "lifelong process" of the prayer of examen. As we
pray it daily, we may perceive more clearly the things "that inhibit

us" from what our hearts most deeply desire: "developing an intimate relationship with the Lord Jesus." Increasingly we will seek "to release from our grasp" all that limits our spiritual freedom and so to grow in love of the Lord. Examen becomes indispensable in our lives when "we understand *the importance of opening our hearts*" to the God whose "still small voice" ceaselessly calls us to inexhaustible newness of life.

Bernardin's words reflect what is probably our own experience as well:

> Still, letting go is never easy. I have prayed and struggled constantly to be able to let go of things more willingly, to be free of everything that keeps the Lord from finding greater hospitality in my soul or interferes with my surrender to what God asks of me.... My daily prayer is that I can open wide the doors of my heart to Jesus and his expectations of me. (6–7)

This is the heart itself of the examen: to seek unceasingly "to be free of everything that keeps the Lord from finding greater hospitality in my soul," from everything that "interferes with my surrender to what God asks of me." It is a "daily prayer" that "I can open wide the doors of my heart to Jesus."

Finally, Bernardin speaks of the *self-emptying* (Phil. 2:7) that frees our hearts to surrender to God:

> God speaks very gently to us when he invites us to make more room for him in our lives. The tension that arises comes not from him but from me as I struggle to find out *how* to offer him fuller hospitality and then to *do* it wholeheartedly. The Lord is clear about what he wants, but it is really difficult to let go of myself and my work and trust him completely. The first step of letting go, of course, is linked with my *emptying* myself of everything — the plans I consider the largest as well as the distractions I judge the smallest — so that the Lord can really take over. (15–16)

God does indeed speak "very gently" to us when "he invites us to make more room for him in our lives." Our hearts need to be finely attuned and daily attentive to hear the voice of that loving invitation. That is why, as we have said from the beginning, the prayer of examen is at the *heart* of the spiritual life. So much depends on hearing the promptings of a God who speaks "very gently" in calling us forward on our spiritual journey.

As Bernardin notes, "the Lord is clear about what he wants." Our struggle, like Bernardin's, is "to find out how" to respond and then "to do it wholeheartedly." To *find out* daily, and then to *do:* this is a powerful description of the prayer of examen.

"Love needs no cause outside itself"

In the end, it all comes down to footprints in the sand: day after day, year after year, in the times when our hearts are warm with God's love and all that is spiritual delights us, and in the times when we must plod forward faithfully under the burning sun and across the miles that seem to stretch endlessly before us, knowing that God sees and loves *each footprint* of our fidelity.[8]

And the energy that impels us forward on that journey is always the same: "We have come to *know* and to *believe* in the love God has for us" (1 John 4:16).[9] What we seek, then, year after year in our examen is "to know the Lord interiorly...so that I may love him more and follow him more closely" (*SpirEx,* 104).

Bernard of Clairvaux, whose faithful love for the Lord transformed hearts and blessed nations, proclaims:

> Love suffices unto itself, gives delight of itself and because of itself. Love is its own merit, its own reward. Love needs no cause outside itself, no fruit other than itself. Its fruit is its practice. I love because I love; I love that I may love. Love is a great thing, so long as it reverts to its source, returns to its origins and flows back to its fount, constantly drawing there the water that gives it new life.[10]

There is finally no other reason why we pray the examen:
"Love needs no cause outside itself. . . . I love because I love; I
love that I may love." That love remains young, fresh, and alive
when, as Bernard says, it continually "flows back to its fount,
constantly drawing there the water that gives it new life." When
that living water flows constantly in our hearts (John 7:38), then
the Spirit guides our lives. In our faithful prayer of examen, we
hear that Voice daily and with our lives we answer: "Lead Thou
me on."

PART FIVE

FRUIT

Chapter Thirteen

Examen and the Community

Martin, Martin! Look out into the street
tomorrow, for I will come.

— Leo Tolstoy: "Where Love Is, God Is"

The fruit of Ignatius's examen

In this chapter we will return yet again to Ignatius's *Spiritual Diary* to ask a simple question: What difference did the practice of examen make for Ignatius on that March 12, 1544? What gift did God give Ignatius through his prayer of examen on that day? What were the *spiritual fruits* of his examen?

We have seen the answers throughout this entire book. As Ignatius prayerfully reviews his day, he notes his experiences of spiritual consolation and spiritual desolation. He is thus able to grasp the meaning of both. His *spiritual consolation,* especially that which follows his time of struggle, confirms his decision as truly of God.[1] Thus Ignatius gains clarity regarding how to proceed in a matter of importance for himself and his companions. He is also equipped to resist any future attempt of the enemy to sway him from this course. Such attempts do in fact arise, and Ignatius quickly and decisively repels them; he remains faithful to the grace given him. The insight and the fidelity to the Spirit's promptings made possible by his examen assist Ignatius in guiding his companions with spiritual surety.

Ignatius's review of his *spiritual desolation* during and after the morning Mass alerts him to a spiritual imbalance in his heart. He examines the cause of his desolation and identifies this in a desire that he knows is not in accord with God's design. Here too, through his examen, Ignatius attains spiritual clarity. Again he recognizes what he must do and acts accordingly. He strives to relinquish that desire, and as he does so the spiritual desolation lifts and consolation returns.

Through attentive examen Ignatius perceives both where God is leading in his day and the promptings of the enemy that oppose that leading. Through his examen Ignatius understands which spiritual stirrings of his heart to accept and which to reject. Because he reviews his spiritual experience Ignatius is able to *find* and to *follow* God unerringly in his day. The prayer of examen breathes spiritual clarity and a capacity for decisive spiritual action into his day. The spiritual fruits of Ignatius's daily examen bless him, his companions, and, through them, the whole People of God.

The fruit of our examen

Those who shared with me their experience of the examen expressed something similar. A woman religious who has prayed the examen for many years says:

> The examen is like a mini-retreat. It helps me to remember what is important. It helps me to get my priorities realigned. Through the examen, I remember the important things: that I'm loveable, that God loves me, that God loved me into creation. I remember the whole point of why I'm here: for God's, my own, and others' happiness. Then I can act out of this awareness during the day.

A married woman speaks of the examen as the prayer of spiritual growth in her life:

> Without the examen I don't know if I'd be able to grow spiritually very easily. This is where I'm aware of how I'm

responding to what's going on in my life. If I'm not responding well, I look to see why. If I feel sad, I try to see why. Through the examen, I notice patterns and trends in my life.

She thinks for a moment and then adds this striking sentence: "Without the examen, I would just be *reacting* and not *responding* throughout the day."

In describing her experience, this woman has touched a profound truth about the examen; it is indeed the prayer of *continuing spiritual growth*. God has given all of us great resources for growth in our lives of faith and love. Those resources may lie dormant for a time. We may doubt whether such growth is truly possible for us. The prayer of examen awakens these capabilities, energizes them, and channels them toward that *holiness* to which we are all called and which the power of God's grace can work in our humanity.[2] The examen is the prayer of that "blessed unrest" of which Kierkegaard speaks: the unending search for deeper communion with God, which gives joy and continual freshness to our spiritual lives.[3]

> The prayer of examen breathed spiritual clarity and a capacity for decisive spiritual action into his day.

A priest who has prayed the examen since his years in the seminary says:

I used to struggle with the examen and still do somewhat today. But I find it much more helpful now. I want to finish the day with the sense that I am attending to Jesus and to where he has been in the day, and whether I've missed that in the day. Still, I keep learning more about the examen, and I discuss this with my spiritual director.

A husband and wife pray the examen together and say that often they do not get beyond the first step of gratitude. Yet having expressed together their gratitude for God's work in the day they find it easier to talk about "the tougher things" in their individual experience and in their married relationship. He says that he learns through the examen how to articulate personal and spiritual realities to himself and to others. She nods agreement and adds: "I find myself articulating things to myself. Then I can get to the emotional roots of things. When I can do this, then I can deal with them. Sometimes I do not see it all clearly in one day, but only over time. Today I see something, tomorrow I will see more."

Her husband continues: "Through our examen together, my relationships with God and with my wife become inextricably linked. God's goodness to me and her goodness to me become inextricably linked." She confirms his words from her own experience, and he adds a further thought: "Feeling loved through the prayer of the examen gives me the hope I need to talk about things that could become big problems before they do become big problems." His wife says, simply: "The examen teaches us that we are children of God."

A mini-retreat, a return during the day to the important things, an awareness of being loveable and loved, a spiritual space out of which to act in the day, a prayer of spiritual growth, a process of noticing spiritual patterns and trends in our lives, a way of responding and not merely reacting to the flow of life, a prayer of attending to Jesus and to where he has led in the day, a means of articulating and of dealing with spiritual experience and with relationship in a marriage: these are only some of the many ways in which the extraordinary *fruitfulness* of the daily examen may be expressed.

The daily prayer of examen possesses great potential for spiritual growth. In this chapter and in the next, we will highlight only a few of the many specific ways in which this may occur.

Discerning awareness throughout the day

Our review of Ignatius's *Spiritual Diary* for March 12, 1544, reveals clearly how at this mature stage of his spiritual development examen is not simply a matter of one or two reflective pauses in the day; rather Ignatius's entire day is punctuated with moments of discerning spiritual awareness. Examen has become *a way of life* as Ignatius rises and prays, as he prepares for and celebrates Mass, as he faces his tasks and ponders a decision he must make, as he eats his midday meal and on throughout his entire busy day.

Those who knew Ignatius testify to his constant discerning awareness in these years of his full spiritual maturity. One of these, Jerónimo Nadal, writes that Ignatius was able "to see and contemplate in all things, actions, and conversations the presence of God and the love of spiritual things, to remain a contemplative even in the midst of action."[4] Another, Pedro Ribadeneira, affirms of Ignatius:

> He has always kept this habit of examining his conscience every hour and of asking himself with careful attention how he had passed the hour. If at the end of it he happened upon some more important matter, or a task which prevented this pious practice, he postponed the examen, but at the first free moment, or the following hour, he made up for this delay.[5]

The fruits of Ignatius's ongoing examen grew progressively more abundant as the years passed. One day, near the end of his life, Ignatius called Luis Gonçalves da Câmara and "with the manner of one more deeply recollected than usual," told da Câmara that "his devotion was continually growing, that is, the ease with which he could find God, and now more than ever in his life. And always, and at whatever hour he wished, he could find God."[6] Who can guess the joy of a life so lived?

If we pray the examen faithfully year after year, with all the struggles and consolations this prayer may entail, we will find ourselves taking the first small but richly blessed steps along this same path. The formal times of examen will flow increasingly into the busyness of the day, and we will be more aware of God in the midst of our activity. The opportunities for such brief moments of discerning awareness are countless, and we will begin to find them. As David Townsend aptly writes:

> This might be achieved in many ways. For instance, at the end of a piece of work or conversation, and before attending to something else, there is frequently room for a quick flash of discerning awareness of God's presence and of the person's own responses to that presence during that piece of work or conversation. There is also frequently time to quickly glance at what is ahead the better to dispose oneself to seek and find God in the new task. This might take a few seconds remaining seated at a desk, or it may take a few minutes walking from one building to another, or it could be done driving to an appointment.[7]

As we faithfully pray the examen in formally chosen times during the day, the desire for this type of "quick flash of discerning awareness" grows. After years of praying the examen, a woman religious now finds herself entering "spontaneously" into the examen as she works in her office. When something "feels out of balance" she says,

> I find a moment to stop. Sometimes I make a special prayer, asking God to help me. Sometimes I just become quiet with the Lord to get a sense of what is bothering me. Often I find that I can identify this. I may be unhappy about the way I responded to someone. Then it gets simple. I see what I need to do.

A woman who has prayed the examen for years finds that something similar occurs for her as well. "At times," she says, "in the midst of the busyness I will sense something stirring within. I may not have time at the moment to stop, but I note this. I feel a kind of 'deficit' and know that I need to examine whatever this is. Then, when I am able, I bring this to the examen."

A man who prays the examen daily tells of his habit in such situations of "grabbing the first free moment and stopping to examine what is going on inside. These quick moments with the Lord give me clarity and more peace to continue my activity." A few minutes seated at a desk, walking from one building to another, driving to an appointment, riding an elevator, after a phone call, or while the children are taking their naps: such brief opportunities for "a quick flash of discerning awareness" are never far from us. Through them we begin like Ignatius to "find God" hour by hour in our day. Examen becomes a grace-filled *way of life* for us as well.

Examen and life together

We have already noted how Ignatius's personal practice of examen on March 12, 1544, blessed his companions and, through them, many others. The clarity of decision resulting from his examen permitted Ignatius to lead others very surely toward God. In this a fundamental truth about the examen is at work: we always make our *personal* prayer of examen within the context of the *Church* and of the *world*. The gift God gives us individually through the examen empowers us to love and serve others with increased spiritual wisdom and strength: our spouses, our children, our community members, our fellow priests, our parish, those we serve in ministry, those we encounter in the workplace, those with whom we share social responsibilities, and all those we meet in the calling God has given us.

A married woman says of her prayer of examen: "I value it immensely because it helps me see my experience and how it connects to God. The examen connects my home life, my work, and all of my life with my spiritual life: the Mass, the rosary, and all my prayer."

This woman actively participates in the life of her parish. She describes a time of anxiety in the parish when no one could be sure whether the parish would have the necessary resources to continue a valued program. She brought this anxiety to her prayer of examen. The examen gave her greater peace and a confidence that the Lord would assist the parish in its need. She tells of perceiving how her greater trust strengthened her pastor also and helped him to face the situation with renewed hope. She saw him take new initiatives toward finding resources for the program. This is always the sign of authentic examen: our personal prayer of examen becomes a gift to others and strengthens the Church.

> If, in our diverse callings, we pray the examen, we will become increasingly a source of such blessing for each other, for the Church, and for the world.

A woman religious speaks of how her examen has blessed her relationships with her sisters in community. She says:

As the examen teaches me more how deeply I am loved by God, it changes the way I see the other sisters as well. Before I related to them above all by asking: "What can I *do* for you?" or "What can you *do* for me?" Or I simply related to them through natural connections — some of us think the same way and some of us do not. Now, though, that is beginning to change. Now, because I know more fully how much God loves me, I see how much God loves the others too and how God is present in them. When something a sister does bothers me, it is easier now to understand that probably she too is making a sincere effort. I feel myself called to be with each sister in her woundedness. I find myself looking for God in the ones who are the "least" for me, those whom I find difficult.

She explains that the word "least" has Gospel meaning for her: to love and serve Jesus in serving the "least" ones in the kingdom (Matt. 25:40).

A man relates his habit of bringing events in the world into his examen. When he watches the news on television or reads the papers he asks: "Do I just feel awful about this, or is there more here?" These events become part of his examen and he says to the Lord: "Are you asking anything of me through this event? Is there anything you want me to do about what I have heard in the news today?" A woman tells of how she brings her family life and the world news of the day to her examen and asks: "Lord, is there anything you want me to do about what is happening around me?"

A married woman, the mother of four young children, relates her experience of what she calls "the family examen." She writes:

For the last several years my husband and I have introduced the Examen as part of our evening meal with our four children (ages thirteen, ten, seven, and four). Using a very simple adaptation of the Examen we pose these two questions: What have you been most grateful for today? What have you been least grateful for today?

The sharing of our responses to these two questions becomes the material for our dinner table discussion. Each member is given a turn to respond to the questions with the other members of the family listening respectfully (on this point we try!). What has struck me about the practice of the Examen in this context is the enthusiasm with which the children participate. It is often the children who initiate the sharing before the adults. It has certainly shaped our dinner-time sharing into something different from what it would be without the focus of these particular questions. It places our day's experience in the context of gratitude and allows us to share both the parts that have positive meaning for us and those that were difficult. It often surprises me what each of the children will choose to share, often not what I thought would have been the focus of the sharing at all. It encourages us to listen to each other, and at times to be challenged to listen more than superficially. It also helps the children to learn to get in touch with their inner experience, and to learn to share that with others.[8]

She continues:

It is difficult to measure the benefit of practicing a family Examen, yet it has proven to be a cherished part of our family life. I believe it has helped to foster a sense of gratitude in each of us. My hope is that it prompts us to be more aware of the presence of God in our daily activities and encourages us to share that awareness with others, even when it is difficult to do so. One of the benefits of doing the Examen communally is that we are encouraged to do it even when, left to our own devices, we would "skip it." This feeling often comes at a time when there is something difficult that has surfaced. We resist "conscious acceptance" of our experience. Taking our turn around the table at such a time can be a source of healing and insight.[9]

The examen is a prayer of *personal* encounter with God that reaches out and blesses the *entire People of God.* If, in our diverse callings, we pray the examen, we will become increasingly a source of such blessing for each other, for the Church, and for the world. The examen of each one will strengthen the other in an endlessly multiplying spiral of grace. May we not dream for a moment of such a Church and of such a world?

Chapter Fourteen

The Examen and Choices

*Church bells beyond the stars heard, the soul's blood
The land of spices; something understood.*
— George Herbert, "Prayer"

"I come to do your will"

When Ignatius first mentions the examen in his Spiritual Exercises, he tells us that its purpose, like that of all the other exercises, is "to seek and find the divine will" in our lives (*SpirEx*, 1). On that March 12, 1544, this is clearly why Ignatius reviews his spiritual experience: to *seek and find God's will* in the decision at hand.

To love the One who loves us is to say like Jesus, "Behold, I come to do your will, O God" (Heb. 10:7). These words, which Jesus proclaims as he comes into the world (Heb. 10:5), are the response of his heart and his life to the Father who says to him: "You are my beloved Son" (Luke 3:22). When our hearts know that they are infinitely loved, that like Jesus and in Jesus *they are beloved*, then the thirst for communion of will and life with God is born. Then our hearts desire to "seek and find the divine will" every day of our lives. As we have observed, there is profound wisdom and spiritual truth in Ignatius's choice to place awareness of God's loving gifts at the beginning of his prayer of examen; the desire to say "yes" to love arises within us when we experience that love concretely.

Because differing voices speak within our hearts (*SpirEx*, 32), a discerning awareness of which promptings are of God and which

169

are not is crucial when we desire "to find the divine will" in daily living. In the preceding chapter we heard one person say: "The examen is like a mini-retreat." This person is exactly right. The examen is *in daily life* that search for God's will that is the goal of the entire Ignatian Spiritual Exercises.

A woman tells of realizing in her examen that she and another woman with whom she worked were "bouncing off each other too much." She recognized that they needed to sit down and talk. She decided in her examen to invite the other woman out for coffee, knowing that in the past such conversations had resolved differences and brought them closer. Through her examen, she has sought and found what God desires in her relationship with another.

A religious priest who regularly prays the examen says that he finds the examen especially helpful when faced with choices of importance. This priest describes how his provincial (religious superior) asked him to discern whether he would wish to continue or to change the ministry in which he was engaged at the time. His spiritual director suggested that he note his thoughts and feelings regarding both options as he made his daily examen. The priest says: "It was a data-collecting time." Then in his meetings with his director he would discuss the thoughts and feelings, the spiritual "data" that emerged from the examen. "In the end," he says, "I came to the point where I knew clearly which option I desired, and I was able to express this to the provincial. At the same time, I felt completely free to accept whatever decision the provincial would make."[1] Both his personal clarity and his openness to the provincial's decision are signs of the authenticity of this man's process of discernment through daily examen.

A woman speaks of her practice of journaling in her examen and says: "I find it easy to journal. Others don't. I've done it all my life. It helps me name what I'm feeling." "And," she adds, "one of the biggest strengths of this is going back over the journal, especially for decision making. I can look back and see the movement." She tells of how she reviews her journal in preparation for her meetings with her spiritual director and describes one time in particular when the prayer of examen helped her to find God's will regarding further studies.

A man tells of facing a "small" decision within his family. For some time he had considered writing to a relative whom he sensed would appreciate the communication. But he was unsure of what to do. He was nervous about reaching out to this relative, about taking a new step in the family situation involved. Life with all its activity continued. He made his examen daily, and the issue of writing emerged from time to time. He says: "Gradually I became convinced that the Lord wanted me to take this step, and I decided that I would write to her. An evening came when I had the time, and I knew that this was the opportunity the Lord was giving me. I wrote to her that evening. I found myself with a peaceful heart that day and the next. I knew that it was a good decision and that she would appreciate my words." Her grateful response some weeks later confirmed the rightness of his action. In this setting too, the life of a family, the examen has helped a person "to seek and find the divine will."

As we have seen, the Jesuit tradition esteems "the examination of conscience...which, in accord with Ignatius's intent, contributes so much to *discernment regarding our entire apostolic life,* to purity of heart, and to familiarity with God in the midst of an active life."[2] Our apostolate, our service to God in our specific calling, may be more or less structured, more or less clear each day, depending on the circumstances of our lives. Still, all of us must often choose one activity rather than another, must decide where the priority in God's service lies today, this week, this year, or for the years to come: Does God desire that I spend time with this child today? Does the Lord will that I dedicate my energy to this task today, or to another? Is the Lord calling the parish to take this particular initiative in the coming year? Is God inspiring me to say "yes" to the offer I received earlier this week? To take the step that I have been considering for some time? In all such cases, the examen truly "contributes so much to discernment regarding our entire apostolic life." This prayer is the space in which we hear with clarity the call of the Lord.

Earlier we quoted one person's remark that "without the examen, I would just be reacting and not responding throughout the day." The examen gives us the insight and the freedom we need to *respond* to God's leading in our lives rather than react unreflectively to the flow of daily events. Whether in "small" matters, such as resolving tensions or communicating with a family member, or in the larger decisions in life, the examen allows us to "collect" the spiritual "data" we need to find the Lord's will each day.[3] Then we truly respond to God and we say with Jesus *in our daily lives:* "Behold, I come to do your will, O God."

Progressive clarification

At times when we pray our examen, the clarity we seek may emerge only after some days, weeks, or months. In the last chapter we heard one woman say: "Sometimes I do not see it all clearly in one day, but only over time. Today I see something, tomorrow I will see more." For Ignatius, March 12, 1544, is the fortieth day in a process of seeking light for a single decision. Frequently God asks of us a love that is patient (1 Cor. 13:4) as we seek the answers we need through faithful examen.

One woman describes a situation that caused her sadness; she feared that many people would be hurt in this matter. She brought her sadness to her examen. As she prayed, she thought of one initiative she could take that would help in a small way to alleviate the situation. She found that this clarity lightened her sadness a little, without removing it entirely. Then she turned to the Lord and said: "Though this looks so negative, I trust that your hand will be at work in this." This act of faith also strengthened her, though something of the sadness still remained. She says: "Things don't necessarily end with just one examen."

No, things do not necessarily end with just one examen. Often the richest fruits of our examen will emerge from many daily examens together as a whole, some prayed with greater and some with less attentiveness and spiritual feeling. As many of the people we have quoted indicate, it is through persevering examen that we gradually perceive the spiritual patterns that reveal where God is leading in our lives.

Finding God in all things

The examen is a process; it develops over time. We begin by praying the examen in a certain way and, if we persevere, it deepens and simplifies. We have seen this growth in Ignatius, who from hesitant beginnings progressively developed the profound spiritual sensitivity revealed on March 12, 1544. His growth like ours was gradual.

The wonder of grace is that faithful perseverance in the examen born of a love that continually "returns to its origins, and flows back to its fount, constantly drawing there the water that gives it new life" (Bernard of Clairvaux), bears fruit beyond what we could have guessed when we first began the journey of examen. We not only gain spiritual clarity regarding specific questions day by day, but also, with the years, another form of more general clarity develops; this gift of grace is one of the most beautiful spiritual blessings we can experience in life.

After years of attentiveness to God's leading day by day, a time comes when the widely diverse experiences of our lives, some painful and confusing at the time, acquire a more comprehensive meaning. We begin to see, just a little, the great patterns of God's workings in our lives. And with this insight a deep gratitude and an almost unshakeable serenity arise in the human heart. One woman's witness to this blessed fruit of the examen is perhaps the most fitting conclusion to our reflections in this book.

This woman is in her seventies. She is physically frail and suffers from an illness that can be alleviated but not cured. She has learned long ago to accept such things in life. Often, with a smile, she will quote the words of Julian of Norwich: "All will be well, and all will be well, and all manner of things will be well." She gives hope to others.

The early years of her family life were a mixture of happiness and tragedy, and she bears still both the gift and the burden of those years. She is talented, intelligent, and capable. She has always done well professionally. She marvels at the friends who have surrounded her in her lifetime. She has known years when God seemed very close and times of spiritual darkness when God seemed far away. There were years of deep interior pain that no one saw.

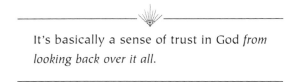

It's basically a sense of trust in God *from looking back over it all.*

She has always been reflective but has striven in a special way for the past thirty years to understand herself and God's workings in her life. She lets nothing deter her from this search. Even the painful times, once the first emotions have subsided sufficiently, become valued times of a learning process that never ends. Daily, constantly, in all that happens around her and in her, she searches for God's word to her, for God's leading in her life. Each evening she reviews her life with God.

Gradually prayer has changed for her. She maintains her daily times of prayer as her health permits. But, she says, in recent years prayer has become a way of life. She lives with God, aware of God, sharing with God. The deep peace that characterizes her now even in the not infrequent struggles of life reveals that this is so.

She tells of a time not many years ago when she was sitting by the sea. Suddenly she found herself reviewing her entire life, remembering the painful and the happy times over the years and to the present. A great sense of gratitude welled up in her heart as she remembered; in that experience of grace, she could see the love of God in *all of this*. Joy and deep peace filled her heart in that moment. She grasped in a new way the meaning of her whole life. A daily effort of over thirty years to perceive God's workings in her life bore fruit in a rich understanding of the pattern of her entire life. She says:

> I feel as though I've turned a corner spiritually in recent months. All the stages of my life have come together. I can see the Lord's love and invitation in each, constantly calling me forward. I've always wanted to be a transparent instrument for the Lord to work through me. It's like he took a Brillo pad and scrubbed me — as I asked. This is truly "awesome." It's basically a sense of trust in God from looking back over it all. I think heaven is this — a constant journey, always discovering God more.

All that we have seen in this book is summarized here: "It's basically a sense of trust in God *from looking back over it all*." This basic "sense of trust in God" that results from faithful review of our spiritual experience over many years is the fruit to which examen finally leads. This kind of trust becomes unshakeable.

At one point this woman had suffered a loss in her life and her heart was heavy. Some days later she went to share in a gathering of her neighbors. About thirty people were already there when she walked into the room. The sun was pouring through the windows. And, as she entered, she saw all of the faces turn toward her. There were many smiles; they were glad to see her. She says: "Suddenly I realized that each one of them was a channel of God's presence to me. I realized that each one was a sign of God's goodness and love for me."

Of another time she writes:

> Yesterday I had a most delightful experience. As I was walking back from the laundry, I was facing that very strong

northwest wind. Once inside again, I realized that my body
was tight with tension and I wondered why. Didn't take long
to figure out that I had been all scrunched up against the
cold wind. Yesterday's reading from the Book of Wisdom
[Wisd. 13] about how the greatness and beauty of nature
should lead one to recognize the hand of the Creator popped
into my head. I can't find the words to express the enormous
delight I felt in realizing that God is very much present in the
cold wind. Frost and chill, bless the Lord [Dan. 3]. Maybe
Ignatius would be pleased that I am continuing to find God
present in all things.

Yes, I think Ignatius would be pleased that her daily search for
God's presence has led her to find God present *in all things:* in the
sun pouring into a room filled with friends, in their welcoming
smiles, in the creation that surrounds her, in all the painful and
joyful stages of her life. I think God must thrill with delight to
see a heart so alive to the divine presence always with her and
so able to grasp that presence. I think God's heart must rejoice
whenever the prayer of examen leads a human heart, as George
Herbert says, to *"something understood."*

That is the grace of the examen. Poet Jessica Powers writes:

> Deep in the soul the acres lie
> of virgin lands, of sacred wood
> where waits the Spirit.[4]

The prayer of the examen introduces us into those depths of
the soul, into that sacred space "where waits the Spirit." This
road lies open to us all. We need only walk in prayer into that
place where the Spirit waits within. The divine love, the clarity,
and the joy that we will find in those "acres . . . of virgin lands"
will bless us every day on our spiritual journey.

Notes

Foreword

1. Timothy Gallagher, O.M.V., *The Discernment of Spirits: An Ignatian Guide for Everyday Living* (New York: Crossroad, 2005).
2. Tim Muldoon, "Postmodern Spirituality and the Ignatian Fundamentum," *The Way* 44 (2005): 94.

Introduction

1. Maureen Conroy, R.S.M., *The Discerning Heart: Discovering a Personal God* (Chicago: Loyola University Press, 1993), 62.

Chapter One / Discovering the Examen

1. George Aschenbrenner, S.J., "Consciousness Examen," *Review for Religious* 31 (1972): 14–21.
2. Ibid, 14.
3. Emphasis added.
4. Throughout this book Ignatius's *Spiritual Exercises* are abbreviated as *SpirEx*. The translation of quotations from the *Spiritual Exercises* is the author's own, from the early Spanish version entitled the Autograph and authoritatively published in *Monumenta Historica Societatis Jesu*, vol. 100, 140–416.

Chapter Two / A Day with Ignatius

1. *Autobiography,* no. 16. Author's translation from the Spanish in Ignacio Iparraguirre, S.J., and Candido de Dalmases, S.J., eds., *San Ignacio de Loyola: Obras Completas* (Madrid: Biblioteca de Autores Cristianos, 1982), 99-100. For Ignatius's complete Autobiography in English, see Joseph O'Callaghan, trans., *The Autobiography of St. Ignatius of Loyola with Related Documents* (New York: Harper & Row, 1974).
2. *Autobiography,* chap. 3.
3. Author's translation, from the text of Ignatius's *Spiritual Diary,* in Iparraguirre and de Dalmases, *San Ignacio de Loyola: Obras Completas,* 380–83. In translating I have utilized the rendering of Ignatius's sometimes difficult text into more readable Spanish by Santiago Thió de Pol, S.J., *La Intimidad del Peregrino: Diario Espiritual de San Ignacio de Loyola* (Bilbao: Mensajero, 1990), 169–75. An English version of this text, as translated by William Young, S.J., is published in Simon Decloux, S.J., *Commentaries on the Letters and Spiritual Diary of St. Ignatius Loyola* (Rome: Centrum Ignatianum Spiritualitatis,

1982), 50–52. Details beyond those given here regarding the *Spiritual Diary* and the significance within it of March 12, 1544, may be found in these sources. The page numbers at the end of each quotation in my text are taken from the edition of the *Spiritual Diary* in *Obras Completas*.

4. The letter dates from the early months of 1544. References are from this letter as published in *Monumenta Historica Societatis Jesu, Epistolae et Instructiones,* I, n. 76, 285–91. Author's translation.

5. These persons include the pope, kings, and members of highly influ-ential families who, for different reasons, are at odds with each other. Thus Ignatius strives to make peace "between Paul III and John III of Portugal in 1542; between Ascanio Colonna and his wife, and between both of these and the pope in 1543." Santiago Thió de Pol, *La Intimidad del Peregrino,* 26.

6. Pedro di Ribadeneira, quoted in Miguel Angel Fiorito, "La vida espir-itual de San Ignacio segùn su Diario Espiritual," *Boletín de Espiritualidad* 57 (1978): 10.

7. See *SpirEx,* 147, the Triple Colloquy, in which Ignatius asks the intercession of Mary with her Son, and of the Son with the Father.

8. Most likely Ignatius's desire for this kind of consolation in the Mass was not merely a self-centered desire for consolation — though something of this may have been at work — but was born of his sense of the importance of this discernment regarding poverty, and the great need he felt to be solidly confirmed by God in a decision with far-reaching consequences for himself and his companions, present and future. Nonetheless the fact remains that he had set his heart on a precise kind of confirmation and had not been simply open to whatever manner of confirmation the Lord would choose to give (*SpirEx,* 154).

9. *SpirEx,* 175–88. "Election," as Ignatius uses the word here, indicates the prayerful process by which persons come to see and to embrace God's will in their lives.

10. To be aware, to understand, to act: this is the threefold paradigm of Ignatian discernment of spirits (*SpirEx,* 313). See Timothy Gallagher, O.M.V., *The Discernment of Spirits: An Ignatian Guide for Everyday Living* (New York: Crossroad, 2005), prologue, for a discussion of these three steps.

Chapter Three / First Step: Gratitude

1. *Autobiography,* nos. 10–11.

2. Ibid, 27. Author's translation. See especially nos. 28–30, where Ignatius narrates several particularly notable experiences of grace.

3. To Inés Pascual. Iparraguirre and de Dalmases, *San Ignacio de Loyola: Obras Completas,* 613. Author's translation.

4. To the priests and scholastics in Coimbra, Portugal. Ibid., 680. Author's translation.

5. Thus, in the Scriptures, Israel is constantly enjoined to *remember* the loving gifts of God in its history as a people, and so find renewed spiritual energies (Deut. 5:15; Ps. 103:2; Ps. 143:5; etc.). Céline, the sister of Thérèse of Lisieux, notes that Thérèse one day said to her: "Gratitude is the thing

that brings us the most grace. . . . I have learnt this from experience; try it, and you will see." Christopher O'Mahoney, O.C.D., ed. and trans., *St. Thérèse of Lisieux by Those Who Knew Her: Testimonies from the Process of Beatification* (Huntington, IN: Our Sunday Visitor, 1975), 138. Ignatius invites us to reflect on God's gifts "with great affection" (*SpirEx,* 234), thus highlighting the involvement of the heart in contemplating God's gifts.

     6. To Simón Rodrigues, March 18, 1542. Ignatius urges Rodrigues to assist King John III of Portugal in making peace with Pope Paul III and asks Rodrigues to do this in gratitude for the king's good will to the Society of Jesus in Portugal. See Iparraguirre and de Dalmases, *San Ignacio de Loyola: Obras Completas,* 679.

     7. *por ser ella desconocimiento.*

     8. *el conocimiento.*

     9. Ibid., 679–80. Author's translation.

     10. Letter of Ignatius to Antonio Brandão, June 1, 1551.

     11. See Louis Savary, S.J., "The Thanksgiving Examen," *Review for Religious* 39 (1980): 238–46.

Chapter Four / Second Step: Petition

     1. Ignatius uses two verbs in outlining the second point of the examen (*SpirEx,* 43). We ask for the grace to *conocer* (to know) and to *lanzar* (to cast from ourselves, to become free of). "Knowledge, as an object of Ignatian petition, is never an end in itself, but is always a means to moving to freedom." Donald St. Louis, "The Ignatian Examen," in *The Way of Ignatius Loyola: Contemporary Approaches to the Spiritual Exercises,* ed. Philip Sheldrake, S.J. (St. Louis: Institute of Jesuit Sources, 1991), 157. The author points to *SpirEx,* 104, 139, and 223.

Chapter Five / Third Step: Review

     1. As in chapter 2 above, the quotations are from Ignatius's *Spiritual Diary* in Iparraguirre and de Dalmases, *San Ignacio de Loyola: Obras Completas,* 380–83. Author's translation.

     2. "Spiritual consolation," as Ignatius employs the term, signifies warm, uplifting affective movements with respect to faith and relationship with God (*SpirEx,* 316). There are, Ignatius says, Spirit-inspired thoughts born from such affective movements (*SpirEx,* 317).

     3. The term "spiritual desolation" indicates the affectively heavy experiences with regard to faith and relationship with God that are the contrary of spiritual consolation (*SpirEx,* 317). As the modifier "spiritual" indicates, these two terms, "spiritual consolation" and "spiritual desolation" refer respectively to affective warmth and heaviness not simply in general, but specifically with respect to the life of *faith.* I have discussed spiritual consolation and spiritual desolation more at length in *The Discernment of Spirits,* chapters 3 and 4.

     4. In describing those affective movements and thoughts that tend of themselves to distance us from God's will, Ignatius most commonly speaks of "the

bad spirit" or "the enemy" (*SpirEx*, 313–36). By "the bad spirit" or "the enemy" Ignatius understands the personal angelic being biblically called "the tempter" (Matt. 4:3). "The word further signifies the *weakness of our humanity* as this tends to hold us back in various ways from moving toward God. Together with all the richness of what it means to be human we are aware that some stirrings of our humanity, unless resisted, will distance us from God. . . . Yet another source of such movements is *the world around us,* the society and culture in which we live and which affect us daily in significant ways. We are blessed to live in a world filled with goodness and wonder, the gift of the Creator to us all. Yet we are also aware that there is a 'world' around us to which, as disciples of Jesus, we 'do not belong' (John 17:14–16). Stirrings may be awakened in our heart by contact with this 'world' that, again, if not resisted, will lead us away from God. The description of these various sources of God-opposed movements articulates our common experience: when we seek to move toward God, together with the saving power of grace, we experience other interior movements caused from within or without that tend to restrain our progress. The different causes of such movements, taken together, comprise the 'enemy' of our spiritual progress." Timothy Gallagher, O.M.V., *The Discernment of Spirits: An Ignatian Guide for Everyday Living* (New York: Crossroad, 2005), 33–34.

5. Susan had not yet found the *cause* of her spiritual desolation as the day began and we may hope that in future examens she will discover more about the causes of any subsequent experiences of spiritual desolation (*SpirEx*, 319). If she does, Susan is more likely to resist such spiritual desolation in its very origins and before it can take hold upon her heart. "The examination he [Ignatius] has in mind is not merely a matter of knowing sins and mistakes, though it does include that. It is, rather, a matter of noting thoughts and affections of all sorts which constitute or affect spiritual life. We need to understand what are the sources of this desolation, why we feel sad, disturbed, and discouraged, how the evil spirit is deceiving us through false premises or bad reasoning or through feelings that generate untrue thoughts. Such self-knowledge . . . enables us to know how best to counterattack the desolation." Jules Toner, S.J., *A Commentary on Saint Ignatius's Rules for the Discernment of Spirits: A Guide to the Principles and Practice* (St. Louis: Institute of Jesuit Sources, 1982), 168.

6. Some, as they progress in love of the Lord, may also need to watch for experiences of deceptive spiritual consolation, a spiritual energy toward goals other than those the Lord desires (*SpirEx*, 328–36).

7. If, as we make this daily review, one specific call to growth should emerge as primary, we may consider addressing this call through the prayer Ignatius entitles the "particular examen" (*SpirEx*, 24–31). See George Aschenbrenner, S.J., "Consciousness Examen," *Review for Religious* 31 (1972): 18–19. The particular examen is a further mode of Ignatian examen, intimately related to that which is the subject of this book, and merits a separate and more complete treatment than is possible within the specific focus of these pages.

Chapter Six / Fourth Step: Forgiveness

1. Jean Vanier, *Community and Growth* (New York: Paulist Press, 1996), 313. The title of the original makes this point with great emphasis: "*La Communauté: Lieu du Pardon et de la Fête*," that is, "Community: The Place of Forgiveness and Celebration."

2. Ibid., 36.

3. As Fiorito observes, Ignatius follows this pattern in the Spiritual Exercises as a whole. His retreatants do not consider what hinders them from responding to God's love (the First Week) until they have first experienced the embrace of that love (Principle and Foundation). And, within the First Week, they do not consider personal sinfulness (Second Exercise) until they have first experienced themselves as loved by the Redeemer (First Exercise, colloquy). See Miguel Angel Fiorito, "La conciencia y su examen," *Stromata* 35, no. 1/2 (1979): 13–15.

4. Further writing on our image of God and its impact on our prayer may be found in William Barry, S.J., *God and You: Prayer as a Personal Relationship* (New York: Paulist Press, 1987), and also, by the same author, *Paying Attention to God: Discernment in Prayer* (Notre Dame, IN: Ave Maria Press, 1990).

5. M. H. Abrams, ed., *The Norton Anthology of English Literature* (New York: W. W. Norton, 1979), 1340–41. The explanatory notes in the text of the poem are taken from this Anthology.

6. "Backward." Ibid., 1340.

7. "The first question of shopkeepers and tavern waiters to an entering customer would be 'What d'ye lack?' (i.e., want)." Ibid., 1341.

8. Spiritual direction greatly facilitates such growth in our image of God and so in the practice of step four of the examen. A related issue of importance is the question of image of *self*, the other person in this relationship, and the impact of this image on our relationship with God. Here too spiritual direction may assist growth.

9. Author's translation, from the text of Ignatius's *Spiritual Diary* in Ignacio Iparraguirre and Candido de Dalmases, *San Ignacio de Loyola: Obras Completas* (Madrid: BAC, 1982), 390–91. See chapter 2 above, with the references to this text given there.

10. In both steps Ignatius employs the same verb: in step two, "*pedir gracia*" (to ask for grace) and in step four, "*pedir perdón*" (to ask for forgiveness). *SpirEx*, 43.

Chapter Seven / Fifth Step: Renewal

1. See above, chapter 2 (p. 48), with the corresponding reference.

2. *proponer enmienda con su gracia*, *SpirEx*, 43.

3. See David Townsend, S.J., "Finding God in a Busy Day," *Review for Religious* 50 (1991): 59, whose article inspired this paragraph. Townsend speaks of this planning as "forearming."

Chapter Eight / Flexibility

1. From "This Trackless Solitude," in *The Selected Poetry of Jessica Powers*, ed. Regina Siegfried, A.S.C., and Robert Morneau (Washington, DC: ICS Publications, 1999), 6.

2. "On reflection, one finds that these five steps actually are the five successive moments in any dynamic movement of personal love: what we always say to a person whom we truly love, in the order in which we want to say it: 1. 'Thank you...' 2. 'Help me....' 3. 'I love you....' 'I really do love you, in spite of the weaknesses and failure in my response....' 4. 'I'm sorry....' 5. 'Be with me.'" Marian Cowan, C.S.J., and John Futrell, S.J., *Companions in Grace: A Handbook for Directors of the Spiritual Exercises of Saint Ignatius of Loyola* (St. Louis: Institute of Jesuit Sources, 2000), 34–35. These five steps are, writes Aschenbrenner, "dimensions of the Christian consciousness, formed by God and His work in the heart as it confronts and grows within this world and all of reality." George Aschenbrenner, S.J., "Consciousness Examen," *Review for Religious* 31 (1972): 16.

3. David Townsend, S.J., "Finding God in a Busy Day," *Review for Religious* 50 (1991): 58. Aschenbrenner writes: "So there is no ideal time allocation for the five elements of the examen each time but rather a daily organic expression of the spiritual mood of the heart. At one time we are drawn to one element longer than the others and at another time to another element over the others." "Consciousness Examen," 16.

4. Jacques Leclercq writes: "We are left with the simplest method, the glance at the soul....How does it stand with me? Is God the one essential for me? Does love of God inspire my whole life? No sooner have we asked this question than the shadows crowd around us showing us the faults which prevent us from being what we wish. And this examination which may be termed a simple look reminds us of the path to be followed while at the same time it revives our desire to belong wholly to God." *The Interior Life* (New York: P. J. Kenedy, 1961), 151. The author sees this form of examen as standing in contrast with the more structured examen as Ignatius gives it. I am suggesting that there is no essential contrast and that the question is more one of development, after suitable grounding, in the practice of examen.

5. Frank Moan, S.J., "In Praise of Horizontal Prayer," *America* 192 (2005): 18–19.

Chapter Nine / The General Setting of the Examen

1. Ignatius outlines the ten additions in *SpirEx*, 73–89, adapts them to the later stages of the Spiritual Exercises in nos. 130, 206, and 229, and asks in nos. 90, 160, and 207 that the retreatant make the particular examen on these additions throughout the Spiritual Exercises.

2. In fact, Ignatius follows precisely this same pattern of spiritual exercise and supplementary additions in describing the particular examen. After outlining the exercise itself of this examen (*SpirEx*, 24–26), he appends four "additions" to it (*SpirEx*, 27–31). We may note that Ignatius allots roughly

equal space both to explaining the steps of this examen and to the additions that he offers as further aids in its practice.

3. George Aschenbrenner, S.J., "Consciousness Examen," *Review for Religious* 31 (1972): 14–21.

4. Jules Toner, S.J., *A Commentary on Saint Ignatius's Rules for the Discernment of Spirits: A Guide to the Principles and Practice* (St. Louis: Institute of Jesuit Sources, 1982), 168. Toner further writes: "It is true that the longer and deeper one's experience of spiritual life, the more one has reflected on it, the more one has grown in spiritual self-knowledge, in spiritual learning, and had experience also of spiritual counseling, both as counselee and counselor, the better can such a one deal with his or her own problems. However, persons who have had the opportunity and capacity for such experience, reflection, counseling, learning, are relatively few; and even they have some need of another to take counsel with. The rest of us have greater need, more or less, the more so the less our learning and experience and the more crucial the matter about which we are concerned. The first and most important step in being open to another is our coming to know reflectively with clarity what is going on in our lives. Very few people can come to this knowledge except by trying to tell someone about it." Ibid., 200–201.

5. One adaptation of this principle consists in praying the examen itself with a spiritual companion. See Gerald E. Keefe, S.J. "The Companion Examen," *Review for Religious* 37 (1978): 59–68. Keefe writes: "The companion examen is the effort of two believers to discern the activity of God in their respective lives and share this with each other" (59).

6. As a reading of Ignatius's *Spiritual Exercises* and, in particular, of his Rules for the Discernment of Spirits (*SpirEx,* 313–36) indicates, Ignatius expects that dedicated people will undergo spiritual struggles at times, and that these lie within the providence of a loving God (*SpirEx,* 320). He sees, therefore, no shame in experiencing such struggles. For Ignatius what *is* crucial is that we respond with spiritual wisdom to these struggles such that they lead to new spiritual growth, as God intends.

7. If this is true, a corollary immediately follows: the great need for spiritual directors conversant with the prayer of the examen and able to instruct and to accompany others in this prayer.

8. "The prayerful quality and effectiveness of the examen itself depends upon its relationship to the continuing contemplative prayer of the person. Without this relationship, examen slips to the level of self-reflection for self-perfection, if it perdures at all." Aschenbrenner, "Consciousness Examen," 15.

9. Ibid., 16.

10. John Veltri, S.J., *Orientations,* vol. 1 (Guelph, Ont.: Loyola House, 1996), 161.

11. Anne Morrow Lindbergh, *Hour of Gold, Hour of Lead: Diaries and Letters of Anne Morrow Lindbergh* (New York: Harcourt Brace Jovanovich, 1973), 261.

12. Henri Nouwen, *Here and Now: Living in the Spirit* (New York: Crossroad, 1994), 76–77.

13. Ibid., 77.

14. I wrote my earlier book, *The Discernment of Spirits: An Ignatian Guide for Everyday Living* (New York: Crossroad, 2005), as an aid to growth in such spiritual awareness.

15. Aschenbrenner, "Consciousness Examen," 16.

16. John Veltri, S.J., offers a set of exercises toward "Developing a Discerning Heart" in *Orientations,* vol. 1 (Guelph, Ont.: Loyola House, 1996), 161–76. These seven "phases" of development, with their corresponding exercises, indicate that such development is indeed "a developed skill" (161). These phases, as Veltri gives them, are the following: (1) acknowledging the different feelings occurring inside oneself, (2) being in touch with the underlying realities behind these feelings, (3) recognizing the biological and psychological origins of one's feelings, (4) recognizing the Christ dimension — or Spirit dimension — in the expression of and in the behavior that flows from one's feelings, (5) recognizing the different ways of God's sharing of self in one's life experiences, (6) recognizing more precisely the spiritual movements in one's being, and (7) using the format of Ignatius of Loyola [the five steps] with the variety of focuses they imply. Spiritual directors may find these helpful either as given in *Orientations* or with some suitable adaptation.

Chapter Ten / The Specific Setting of the Examen

1. Testimony of Diego Laínez, second general of the Society of Jesus. Quoted in Charles O'Neill, S.J., "*Acatamiento:* Ignatian Reverence in History and in Contemporary Culture," *Studies in the Spirituality of Jesuits* 8 (1976): 7.

2. Mirroring his own practice in the testimony just cited, Ignatius also suggests that this awareness of God's gaze upon us be expressed bodily: "making a physical gesture of reverence or humility" (*SpirEx,* 75). This bodily gesture incarnates and completes the heart's awareness of God's loving presence. As with similar Ignatian counsels regarding prayer, this suggestion too may be considered and adopted in the measure that each finds helpful.

3. *Spiritual Canticle,* 19, 6. Author's translation.

4. Some authors see this transition as so central that they consider it the first step itself of the examen. For John Govan, awareness of this presence is the first of four steps in the examen: John Govan, S.J., *The Examen: Living and Growing with Christ,* leaflet, n.d., n.p., 6. See also Miguel Angel Fiorito, S.J., "La conciencia y su examen," *Stromata* 35, no. 1/2 (1979): 20–23. For Fiorito too, this consciousness of God's presence also becomes a separate step of the examen, the first of six steps. See also Robert Marsh, S.J., "Looking at God Looking at You: Ignatius' Third Addition," *The Way* 43 (2004): 19–28.

5. St. Cyprian, bishop, "De Dominica Oratione," in *Corpus Christianorum, Series Latina,* 1976, IIIA, 94. Author's translation. The Liturgy of the Hours follows a similar pattern in both Morning Prayer and Evening Prayer; in both instances, the intercessions conclude with the prayer of the Our Father.

6. In other contexts Ignatius mentions the Hail Mary or the Soul of Christ (*SpirEx,* 63, 147, 248).

7. Julien Green, *Diary,* trans. Anna Green, selected by Kurt Wolft (New York: Harcourt, Brace & World, 1964), 280.

8. Joseph Tetlow, S.J., "The Most Postmodern Prayer: American Jesuit Identity and the Examen of Consciousness, 1920–1990," *Studies in the Spirituality of Jesuits* 26 (1994): 42–43.

9. Martin Buber, *Tales of the Hasidim: The Early Masters* (New York: Schocken Books, 1968), 69.

10. Ignatius does specify a length of time for the review of each hour of prayer in the Spiritual Exercises. This review is to last "for the space of a quarter of an hour" (*SpirEx,* 77). In the first of his "Three Manners of Praying," itself a kind of examen, Ignatius suggests that we reflect on how we have lived each of the commandments, "keeping as a rule the time one takes to pray the Our Father three times and the Hail Mary three times" (*SpirEx,* 241). He immediately adds that this "rule" is to be applied flexibly, according to the points in which a person finds more or less material for prayer (*SpirEx,* 242).

11. Thirty-Second General Congregation, decree 11, no. 38. Quoted in John Padberg, S.J., ed., *The Constitutions of the Society of Jesus and Their Complementary Norms* (St. Louis: Institute of Jesuit Sources, 1996), 261. The editor chooses the text cited here to illustrate the "importance and meaning" of the examen of conscience (p. 438). Other references to the examen in Ignatius's *Constitutions* include nos. 261, 342, and 344. With respect to the Jesuit tradition see also Tetlow, "The Most Postmodern Prayer," 3–6.

12. "*Sp.Exs.* 43 has the five points of the Method of Making the General Examen.... It is implicit that this be at least a twice daily examen: 'an account of my soul from the time of rising up to the present examination' and 'in the same order as was explained under the Particular Examination of Conscience' (*Sp.Exs.* 43).... The 'in the same order' suggests the general examen is to be made at least twice a day and perhaps at the same times as the particular examen.... We are ... told that the particular examen is to be made after dinner and after supper. Perhaps these are also suitable times for making the general examen." David Townsend, S.J., *The Examen Re-examined* (Rome: Centrum Ignatianum Spiritualitatis, 1987), 17–18.

13. Martin Palmer, S.J., *On Giving the Spiritual Exercises: The Early Jesuit Manuscript Directories and the Official Directory of 1599* (St. Louis: Institute of Jesuit Sources: 1996), 190. See also the similar text of the fourth general of the Society, Everard Mercurian: Ibid., 112–13.

14. Ibid., 349. Aschenbrenner, writing in 1972 for those who live the religious life, speaks of "one or two quarter-hour periods in a day," evidently speaking from this same tradition. See "Consciousness Examen," 5. Many religious institutes have formulated their own practice of the examen, often drawing upon Ignatius and his Spiritual Exercises.

15. Joseph Koterski, S.J., *The Ignatian Examen,* leaflet, n.d., n.p. John Wickham, S.J., writes: "The examen prayer should be kept short (otherwise the pray-er will not persevere in it). It could take about ten minutes, and it should not go longer than fifteen minutes." *Prayer Companions Handbook* (Montreal: Ignatian Centre Publications, 1991), 173.

16. As, for example, the Ignatian-inspired Christian Life Communities, which include in their Program of Life "discernment by means of a daily review of one's life." Neither the Program of Life nor the other documents included in

the international Web site for these Communities offer further details regarding the time members will give to the examen. See *www.cvx-clc.net.*

17. In designating times for the daily particular examen, Ignatius opts for the times after the two main meals of the day (*SpirEx*, 25–26) rather than for the final moments before retiring.

18. Lawrence Elliot, *George Washington Carver: The Man Who Overcame* (Englewood Cliffs, NJ: Prentice-Hall, 1966), 200.

19. See Sarah Ban Breathnach, *The Simple Abundance Journal of Gratitude* (New York: Warner Books, 1996).

20. Anne Morrow Lindbergh, *Gift from the Sea* (New York: Pantheon Books, 1955), 9.

21. February 2, 1544–February 27, 1545.

22. *Autobiography*, no. 100. Da Câmara speaks of seeing Ignatius with *un fajo muy grande de escritos*, "a very large packet of written pages." These evidently exceed the twenty-five pages of notes comprising the *Spiritual Diary* as we have it.

23. Iparraguirre and de Dalmases, *San Ignacio de Loyola: Obras Completas*, 338–40; Miguel Angel Fiorito, "La lucha en el Diario Espiritual," *Boletín de Espiritualidad* 59 (1978): 7–8.

24. "Second Directory of St. Ignatius" in Martin Palmer, S.J., *On Giving the Spiritual Exercises: The Early Jesuit Manuscript Directories and the Official Directory of 1599*, 13. See also the counsel of Lawrence Nicolai, S.J., given approximately in the year 1587: "I urge them to note down their holy resolutions, lights, and devout affections, together with the reasons and motives. They should try to express in few words the main point of the whole fruit so that later they can use it to renew their spirit." Ibid., 156. We may also note that in his "additions" to the daily particular examen Ignatius explicitly recommends writing — according to a series of lines — as an aid to this prayer (*SpirEx*, 28–31).

25. José Calveras, S.J., *Práctica de los Ejercicios Intensivos* (Barcelona: Editorial Balmes, 1952), 120. Author's translation.

26. Fiorito, "La conciencia y su examen," 41.

Chapter Eleven / Examen and the Courage to Love

1. Benedicta Ward, trans., *The Sayings of the Desert Fathers* (Kalamazoo, MI: Cistercian Publications, 1975), 89. I have replaced the use of "thou" with "you."

2. See Timothy Gallagher, O.M.V., "The Courage to Be Spiritually Aware," in *The Discernment of Spirits: An Ignatian Guide for Everyday Living* (New York: Crossroad, 2005), 18–20. The courage to seek spiritual awareness is the same courage that permits us to pray the examen.

3. Jean Vanier, *Community and Growth* (New York: Paulist Press, 1996), 120.

4. John Clarke, O.C.D., trans., *St. Thérèse of Lisieux: Her Last Conversations* (Washington, DC: ICS Publications, 1977), 142.

5. I refer above all to the problems that arose in past decades — generally prior to the widespread influence of Aschenbrenner's 1972 article — from a formation in the examen that led, too often, to discouragement in praying it. These issues have been amply documented and explored in recent decades. See Aschenbrenner's article itself; David Townsend, S.J., *The Examen Re-Examined* (Rome: Centrum Ignatianum Spiritualitatis, 1987), 11–15, and the entire essay; Joseph Tetlow, S.J., "The Most Postmodern Prayer: American Jesuit Identity and the Examen of Consciousness, 1920–1990," *Studies in the Spirituality of Jesuits* 26 (1994); Herbert Alphonso, S.J., *Discovering Your Personal Vocation: The Search for Meaning through the Spiritual Exercises* (New York: Paulist Press, 2001), 56–73.

6. *The Ascent of Mount Carmel,* I, 11, 6. Author's translation.

7. In Ignatian terms this is the healing experience of the First Week of the Spiritual Exercises. See *SpirEx,* 53, 61.

8. Emphasis added.

9. When we do not yet feel the desire for complete openness to God, Ignatius counsels us to pray for *the desire itself* (*SpirEx,* 157, 168, 180). All can make this prayer.

10. One experienced retreat director expresses his conviction, in fact, that "the ones who make the examen best are those who have 'bottomed out' in some way in life."

11. Ignatius addresses the specific needs of these persons in the fourteen rules found in *SpirEx,* 313–27.

Chapter Twelve / Examen and Surrendering to Love

1. "There will also be times of calm when neither movement is present. Ignatius describes this experience of the heart in which neither spiritual consolation nor spiritual desolation is present as a 'tranquil time when the soul is not agitated by various spirits and uses its natural faculties freely and tranquilly' (*SpirEx,* 177)." Timothy Gallagher, O.M.V., *The Discernment of Spirits: An Ignatian Guide for Everyday Living* (New York: Crossroad, 2005), 110.

2. *Spiritual Diary,* in Iparraguirre and de Dalmases, *San Ignacio de Loyola: Obras Completas,* 380. Author's translation. The subsequent quotations are from this same source.

3. "Ignatius employs the term *desolation* according to the familiar usage of the word: a condition of affective heaviness that instills sadness and depletes energy for living. The adjective *spiritual* ... signifies that which is directly and immediately referred to faith and the pursuit of God's will. Thus the phrase *spiritual desolation* indicates an affective heaviness (and so 'desolation') directly impacting our faith and pursuit of God's will (and so 'spiritual')." Gallagher, *The Discernment of Spirits,* 60–61. A practical knowledge of Ignatius's Rules of Discernment for the First Week (*SpirEx,* 313–27) is an invaluable help in recognizing and overcoming spiritual desolation.

4. A different, though related issue is the question of *nonspiritual* desolation (bodily tiredness, varying levels of emotional depression), which calls for appropriate remedies on its own level as is clear in the above account of

the man struggling with addiction. Clarity regarding the distinction between spiritual and nonspiritual desolation is crucial in the spiritual life and for spiritual direction in particular. I have discussed this matter in *The Discernment of Spirits*, especially in chapters 4 through 7. When the desolation is *nonspiritual*, depending upon the seriousness of its cause and the level of emotional maturity of the person involved, it may not always be wise for the person to explore the cause of the desolation without competent help.

5. John Henry Newman, "The Pillar of the Cloud," verse two.

6. Joseph Cardinal Bernardin, *The Gift of Peace: Personal Reflections* (Chicago: Loyola Press, 1997), 1–17. The subsequent quotations are from this source.

7. Bernardin describes in this book his own decision, made some twenty years earlier, to dedicate the first hour of each day to prayer. Ibid., 4–6, 96–100.

8. Flannery O'Connor writes: "The only force I believe in is prayer, and it is a force I apply with more doggedness than attention." *The Habit of Being* (New York: Farrar, Straus, Giroux, 1979), 100.

9. Emphasis added.

10. Bernard of Clairvaux, *Sermons on the Canticle of Canticles*, 83, 4. Author's translation.

Chapter Thirteen / Examen and the Community

1. The consolation that Ignatius experiences here is *spiritual* consolation: consolation in God, on the level of faith. Nonspiritual consolation would not serve as an adequate criterion for such discernment. See Timothy Gallagher, O.M.V., *The Discernment of Spirits: An Ignatian Guide for Everyday Living* (New York: Crossroad, 2005), 48–51. Such spiritual consolation is an unambiguous confirmation of God's desire within the dynamic of the rules for discernment of the First Week (*SpirEx, 313–27*). Further discernment regarding the spiritual consolation itself is required in the situation described in the rules for discernment of the Second Week (*SpirEx, 328–36*).

2. This is the universal call to holiness of which the Second Vatican Council speaks: "Therefore all in the Church ... are called to holiness, according to the apostle's saying: 'for this is the will of God, your sanctification' (1 Thess. 4:3; see Eph. 1:4)." *Dogmatic Constitution on the Church*, chapter 5, 39.

3. "Faith means just that blessed unrest, deep and strong, which so urges the believer onward that he cannot settle at ease in this world. . . . For a believer cannot sit still, as a man might sit with a pilgrim's staff in his hand; a believer journeys on." Søren Kierkegaard, *Gospel of Sufferings* (London: James Clarke & Co., 1955), 13.

4. Quoted in Joseph de Guibert, S.J., *The Jesuits: Their Spiritual Doctrine and Practice* (Chicago: Institute of Jesuit Sources, 1964), 45.

5. Ibid., 66. See also the *Memorial* of Luis Gonçalves da Câmara, no. 24, for a similar testimony.

6. *Autobiography*, 99. Author's translation.

7. David Townsend, S.J., *The Examen Re-Examined* (Rome: Centrum Ignatianum Spiritualitatis, 1987), 54.

8. Catherine Macaulay, "The Ignatian Examen: A Contemporary Tool for Awareness and Discernment," thesis for the degree of Master of Arts, Concordia University, Montreal, 2004, 86. Macaulay cites these two questions, "What have you been most grateful for today? What have you been least grateful for today?" as she finds them in Dennis Linn, Sheila Fabricant Linn, and Matthew Linn, S.J., *Sleeping with Bread: Holding What Gives You Life* (New York: Paulist Press, 1995).

9. Ibid., 87.

Chapter Fourteen / The Examen and Choices

1. This complete availability to God's will (in this case as mediated through the vow of religious obedience, in accordance with this man's religious calling) is, Ignatius says, the necessary disposition of heart if we would "seek and find" God's will (*SpirEx,* 23, 169, etc.).

2. Thirty-Second General Congregation, 1975, decree 11, no. 38. Emphasis added.

3. Again, as these stories indicate, much is gained by sharing with a competent spiritual person, especially in decisions of importance.

4. From "This Trackless Solitude," in *The Selected Poetry of Jessica Powers,* ed. Regina Siegfried, A.S.C., and Robert Morneau (Washington, DC: ICS Publications, 1999), 6.

For Further Reading

Aschenbrenner, George, S.J. "Consciousness Examen." *Review for Religious* 31 (1972): 14–21.

———. "A Check on Our Availability: The Examen." *Review for Religious* 39 (1980): 321–24.

English, John, S.J. *Discernment and the Examen.* Guelph, Ont.: Loyola House, 1985.

Gallagher, Timothy, O.M.V. *The Discernment of Spirits: An Ignatian Guide for Everyday Living.* New York: Crossroad, 2005.

Govan, John, S.J. "The Examen: A Tool for Holistic Growth." *Review for Religious* 45 (1986): 394–401.

Keefe, Gerald, S.J. "The Companion Examen." *Review for Religious* 37 (1978): 59–68.

Linn, Dennis, Sheila Fabricant Linn, and Matthew Linn, S.J. *Sleeping with Bread: Holding What Gives You Life.* Mahwah, NJ: Paulist Press, 1995.

Savary, Louis, S.J. "The Thanksgiving Examen." *Review for Religious* 39 (1980): 238–46.

St. Louis, Donald. "The Ignatian Examen." In *The Way of Ignatius Loyola: Contemporary Approaches to the Spiritual Exercises,* ed. Philip Sheldrake, S.J., 154–64. St. Louis: Institute of Jesuit Sources, 1991.

Tetlow, Joseph, S.J. *Choosing Christ in the World: Directing the Spiritual Exercises of St. Ignatius of Loyola according to Annotations Eighteen and Nineteen: A Handbook.* St. Louis: Institute of Jesuit Sources, 1989.

———. "The Most Postmodern Prayer: American Jesuit Identity and the Examen of Conscience, 1920–1990." *Studies in the Spirituality of Jesuits* 26 (1994): 1–67.

Townsend, David Keith, S.J. *The Examen Re-examined.* Rome: Centrum Ignatianum Spiritualitatis, 1987.

———. "Finding God in a Busy Day." *Review for Religious* 50 (1991): 43–63.

Veltri, John, S.J. *Orientations,* vol. 1: *A Collection of Helps for Prayer.* Guelph, Ont.: Loyola House, 1996, 159–76.

———. *Orientations,* vol. 2, Part A: *For Those Who Accompany Others on the Inward Journey.* Guelph, Ont.: Loyola House, 1998, 40–45.

Wickham, John, S.J. *Prayer Companion's Handbook.* Montreal: Ignatian Centre Publications, 1991, 166–79.

Of Related Interest

Timothy Gallager, O.M.V.
THE DISCERNMENT OF SPIRITS
An Ignatian Guide for Everyday Living

By providing a sound understanding of Ignatian principles and applying them in a skillful way to daily life, Father Gallagher meets the pressing needs of retreat directors, retreatants, students of spiritual theology, and others interested in deepening their spiritual lives. I know of no comparable volume that proves so helpful.

— Harvey D. Egan, S.J., Professor of Systematic and Mystical Theology, Boston College (from the foreword)

Although Ignatius of Loyola, founder of the Jesuits, is one of the most influential spiritual leaders of all time, most readers find his Rule hard to understand. Gallagher, an authority and gifted teacher, helps us understand the Rule and how its insights are essential for our spiritual growth today.

0-8245-2291-5, $24.95, paperback

crossroad

Of Related Interest

Dean Brackley, S.J.
THE CALL TO DISCERNMENT
IN TROUBLED TIMES
*New Perspectives on the
Transformative Wisdom of
Ignatius of Loyola*

As the centerpiece of Crossroad's expanding offerings in Jesuit spirituality and thought, we offer this remarkable book from Dean Brackley, a leader in social justice movements and professor in El Salvador. Brackley takes us through the famous Ignatian exercises, showing that they involve not only private religious experience but also a social, moral dimension, including the care for others.

0-8245-2268-0, $24.95 paperback

Check your local bookstore for availability.
To order directly from the publisher,
please call 1-800-707-0670 for Customer Service
or visit our Web site at *www.cpcbooks.com.*
For catalog orders, please send your request to the address below.

THE CROSSROAD PUBLISHING COMPANY
16 Penn Plaza, Suite 1550
New York, NY 10001

All prices subject to change.

crossroad